healthy Eating

foods that fight back

THE AUSTRALIAN Women's Weekly

contents

Good diet, good health: with every passing day we're discovering more and more about how the two are inexorably linked. And when I say "good" diet, I mean both delicious and beneficial toward helping you live longer. The recipes in this book aren't strict or boring, but they are calculated to ensure you eat a sound diet that's low in fat and high in all the necessary nutrients. Add to this that they're also simple to prepare, well-balanced and deliciously appetising, and I feel certain you'll love cooking these recipes, because your meals will be not just good, but GREAT!

Pamela Clark

Food Director

fit & healthy for life

As the saying goes, you are what you eat. And when it comes to living a long and healthy life, it really comes down to you are what you *repeat*. Scientific research has clearly shown that there are patterns of daily eating and exercise habits that are more health promoting than others.

Predictions place 3.5 million of the Australian population over 65 years of age by 2016. And, with the rate of life expectancy increasing, by 2051 it's expected that we will all personally know a centenarian.

When you match this ageing population and escalating health-care costs with the strengthening diet-disease link, it's no surprise that nutrition research resources are being devoted to the anti-ageing cause. The emphasis is now on "ageing successfully" by increasing our quality of life as we live to a riper old age. It's about our health span, not simply life span.

Ask any centenarian about the key to their fountain of youth, and you'll often hear something about their diet. There are many personal theories but, more often than not, it comes back to food, i.e., healthy, nutrient-packed hero foods – foods that promote wellness (see page 22) – and key dietary patterns that see you living a longer, stronger, happier and healthier life.

So, if your wellbeing has been flagging a bit lately, or perhaps you've even had a little health scare, there's no better time to take stock of your diet and lifestyle. Get set to learn about foods that fight back – the ones to assist you in winning life's prizefight.

wellbeing diet principles

keep a healthy weight

The link between being overweight or obese and lifestyle diseases is well established, and your primary goal should be to achieve and maintain a healthy weight. Body weight is all about energy balance, or kilojoules in versus kilojoules out. If you're overweight, a combination of reducing kilojoules from the food you eat plus burning more kilojoules through physical activity is the key to success.

Long-term changes to your exercise and eating habits don't happen overnight. Most people have an extra edge to success when they have a supportive environment and join a formal weight-loss program. For specialised dietary and exercise advice, particularly if you have existing medical problems, see an accredited practising dietitian (in Australia, search for one in your local area at www.daa.asn.au).

Research from a US weight-loss registry has revealed that, even though people followed many different paths to lose weight, they had a number of eating and lifestyle habits in common during the maintenance phase, including eating breakfast and nibbling on healthy snacks (see panels, at right).

did you know?

Phytochemicals are naturally-occurring compounds (other than vitamins and minerals) in plants that enhance our health. They are also known as phytonutrients.

make breakfast a ritual

Nearly 80 per cent of participants on the US weight-loss registry reported eating breakfast every day. Research has shown that, contrary to popular belief, skipping breakfast does not help weight loss. In fact, breakfast eaters are more likely to be within the healthy weight range than breakfast skippers. So, set your alarm clock 15 minutes earlier, stock the pantry and fridge with a range of wholegrain cereals, canned fruit and fat-free yogurt, and get munching.

pack a healthy snack

Participants on the US weight-loss registry commonly ate up to five meals a day. Healthy snacks keep energy levels up between meals, and stop ravenous hunger, so you're less likely to overeat at the main meal. Including appropriate between-meal snacks into your healthy-eating plan is a great way to assist your weight-loss goals. If you're out and about a lot, pack snacks such as grain and fruit-based bars, fresh fruit or fruit snacks in natural juice, dried fruit and nuts, air-popped popcorn or drinking yogurt.

Antioxidants occur naturally in the body. They mop up excess free radicals before they can do any harm. Free radicals are a normal product of metabolism (processes occurring within the body's cells that are necessary for life). However, an excess of free radicals can attack healthy cells, damage healthy DNA and weaken the immune system. They have also been linked to changes that accompany ageing and disease processes that lead to cancer, heart disease and stroke. To slow down the affects of free radicals, it is important to eat plenty of fresh foods that are full of antioxidants (see page 9).

maximise food variety

A healthy diet should include the right amounts of all the food groups every day. This way your body is guaranteed to get the recommended dietary intakes of all the essential vitamins and minerals. Eat a wide variety within the food groups to maximise your intake of protective food components (antioxidants, phytochemicals vitamins and minerals) to enhance your wellbeing.

As a general guide, aim for 30 different types of food a day. It might sound challenging, but with five vegetables, chicken, rice, sesame seeds and fresh ginger you're well on your way with a stir-fry dinner. (Check out the *daily servings and serving sizes* table, page 26).

get the right balance

Sugar adds kilojoules to your diet and not much else. Apart from its enjoyable sweet taste, you're not getting any nutrients or potent antioxidants. But it's a myth that sugar causes diabetes, and it can't be blamed for the obesity epidemic. Sugar was once blamed solely for tooth decay, however, it is now accepted that many different carbohydrate foods, and acids in foods such as orange juice, can lead to dental caries and erosion if they are exposed to teeth for long periods of time. Sugar can certainly improve the palatability of highly nutritious foods like wholegrains, and is fine in moderation, especially if you are a healthy weight.

Fats can be either good or bad, and there's so much information around about fats these days, it's easy to get confused. Many people still need to cut down their total fat, as well as their saturated fat, intake and boost their ratio of healthy fats, including potent omega-3 fatty acids. (See *how much fat should you be getting?*, page 10, for a guide to daily fat requirements.)

Salt is often linked to high blood pressure and kidney disease and, today, most people, whether on medical advice or just for good health, are aware of the dietary guideline to cut down on salt, or sodium chloride. So it's not surprising that we've seen a drop in the use of table salt and salt in cooking, but that doesn't always equate to eating less salt, as about 80 per cent of the salt we now consume is already added to foods.

As well as limiting high-salt foods, such as cheeses, takeaway food, salty snacks and spreads, it pays to watch out for processed foods such as ready-made meals, some canned foods, and Asian and simmer sauces, which can be very high in salt. While it's still fine to consume these foods from time to time, especially if your diet is generally based around lower-salt choices, switch to "salt reduced" or "low salt" brands where possible. Low-salt foods must have less than 120mg sodium/100g.

wholegrains for whole benefit

The Australian Guide to Healthy Eating recommends that a healthy diet for adults should include at least four servings of grain-based foods every day, and at least half of these servings should be wholegrain foods. Wholegrain foods are grain-based foods that contain all three parts, or layers, of the grain – the bran (the outer layer), endosperm (the main part) and germ (the smallest part).

Wholegrain foods have been hailed for their superior nutrition status – like fruit and vegetables they are rich sources of antioxidants. Plus, they provide the body with vitamins (E, B6 and folate), minerals (selenium, copper, iron, zinc, manganese and magnesium), fibre, resistant starch, antioxidants, phytoestrogens and unsaturated fatty acids.

boost your immunity

Your immune system is your body's natural defence mechanism that protects you against attack from foreign substances, such as viruses and bacteria. Immune function declines with age and stress, and lack of sufficient sleep can further deplete your immune system. You can boost your immunity and enhance your wellbeing with the help of the top three immune nutrients – vitamin C, zinc and iron.

Vitamin C really does spell immunity. This potent antioxidant protects the body from free-radical damage and plays an important role in maintaining immune function. Adequate vitamin C may help reduce the severity and duration of the common cold, but there's not great evidence that vitamin C supplements will stop you getting sick in the first place. Go for a daily serving of vitamin C-rich fruit (kiwifruit, especially kiwi gold, has nearly twice the vitamin C of an orange) or juice such as citrus and blackcurrant. There are also plenty of vitamin C-rich vegetables, such as capsicum, especially red capsicum, tomatoes, cabbage, wombok and broccoli. However, some vitamin C is lost in cooking, so eat raw or cook lightly to leave a little crunch.

Zinc is the missing link as this mineral is often neglected when it comes to priorities in dietary advice. However, zinc plays a major role in immunity (as well as sexual function and hair loss). Go for oysters, one of the richest dietary sources, plus three to four servings of lean red meat a week. Wholegrain cereals are also good zinc sources, as are legumes and grainy bread, however, the zinc in these are not as well absorbed as from meat and seafood. Zinc is better absorbed when consumed with a source of animal protein such as dairy.

Iron, as well as boosting energy levels, also plays an important role in immunity. Go for three to four servings of lean red meat a week. Eat plenty of vitamin C-rich foods and herbs, such as parsley, with meals, to help boost the absorption of iron from non-meat sources like green leafy vegetables, iron-fortified breakfast cereals and breads and legumes.

don't forget the fibre

Dietary fibre is one of the key factors to a good working bowel and digestive system, but before you say that's old news, what is new is recognising there's more to fibre than unprocessed bran. There are three different types of fibre that work together to help ensure regular bowel and digestive health – soluble fibre, insoluble fibre and resistant starch. It's just a matter of making sure you eat enough of each type.

Soluble fibre helps slow the digestive process, allowing for maximum absorption of nutrients. It also helps increase the feeling of fullness, called satiety. Good sources include oats and oat-based foods, fruit and legumes.

Insoluble fibre is the fibre that most people know as the one that helps with bowel movements, or elimination. It also helps prevent the build up of waste products and toxins in the body. Foods containing insoluble fibre include wholegrain breads and cereals, vegetables, fruit skins and seeds, and unprocessed bran.

Resistant starch resists digestion in the small intestine and enters the large bowel. It encourages the growth of beneficial bacteria, and produces compounds that help keep the bowel lining healthy. It also helps with elimination. Currently, it is estimated that Australians consume around 3-6g resistant starch per day, which is not enough. Foods naturally high in resistant starch include underripe bananas, cold cooked potato, cold pasta and rice, and legumes such as baked beans. Hi-Maize and inulin are natural ingredients that are added to certain commercial food products, and are very high in resistant starch.

suspect supplements

Scientists are trying to find the active nutrients and other components in hero foods, in order to explore their possible anti-ageing or disease-protecting benefits. And this is where things get a little controversial: studies of diets that have been supplemented with high levels of antioxidants and other extracts from foods, have sometimes failed to repeat the benefits seen from the whole food. It's likely there are complex interactions between the nutrients and antioxidants in whole foods that produce the ultimate beneficial effect, so eating the whole food is still the way to go.

did you know?

Wholegrain foods are receiving even more attention with international research revealing that people who eat wholegrain foods regularly can have a 20 to 40 per cent lower risk of heart disease and stroke compared with those who rarely eat wholegrain foods.

did you know?

Japanese dietary guidelines advise to "make all activities pertaining to food and eating pleasurable ones". Japanese families enjoy home cooking, eat together, and use the mealtime as an occasion for communication.

a bounty of bush foods

Traditional Australian bush foods are finding their way onto supermarket shelves. At home, you can now combine a bush food spice rub, such as lemon myrtle, on your fresh kangaroo meat and top it off with Kakadu plum and chilli sauce. It's been suggested we could all learn a thing or two from primitive hunter/gatherer-type diets and lifestyles (fresh food and plenty of exercise).

functional foods

These are foods that provide health benefits beyond basic nutrition, i.e., they have been shown to affect a specific function or system in the body and may play an important role in disease prevention. The ingredients may be naturally occurring in these foods – such as soluble fibre in oat bran – or the ingredient may be removed or added during processing to boost or lower the levels – such as fat-reduced, calcium-enriched milk.

ageing tastefully

Scientists know that a major determinant as to whether or not you age well is to be found in your genes. But your genes are certainly not your destiny. A healthy lifestyle can influence to what extent your genes determine wellbeing. Scientists are also interested in exploring the ins and outs of healthy lifestyles from regions of the globe that produce their fair share of fit and active older people.

Okinawan odyssey Figures released from the World Health Organisation (WHO) show that the Japanese population live the longest, healthiest lives. The most remarkable thing about the Japanese diet is the wide variety of foods. A study of the diets of 200 elderly Japanese women revealed they ate over 100 biologically different foods each week, while in Australia the average number is more likely around 12 to 15. Research has shown that the greater the variety of foods in the diet, the less risk of many diseases, because you're more likely to get a wider range of protective nutrients, such as antioxidants and phytochemicals.

Okinawa, a Japanese island territory, has more than its fair share of healthy, active centenarians. Like the majority of Japanese, Okinawans eat mainly a plant-based diet with a great variety of vegetables, including seaweeds and other sea vegetables, bamboo shoots, lotus root, spinach, eggplant, various mushrooms, sweet potato and wombok, plus a little fish and soy, and the right amounts of dietary fats.

Green tea is a staple drink that is rich in antioxidants and is also believed to offer digestive wellbeing. Okinawans also enjoy their own unique, ancient hero foods, such as turmeric tea and bitter melon, however, it's their distinct lifestyle habits, including daily physical activity, maintenance of a lifelong healthy weight, self-responsibility for health, and a strong social and community support, which set the islanders apart.

Mediterranean magic As a multicultural country, we have adopted the best of many diverse cultures, including dishes from the Mediterranean region. A greater emphasis on the Mediterranean diet would not only take advantage of our wonderfully fresh foods and plentiful produce, but could benefit the health of all Australians. Research shows that eating a Mediterranean diet can lower the risk of heart and other lifestyle diseases. Roasted red peppers, eggplant and an abundance of fresh vegetables, fruit, fish, nuts and pulses, together with pasta, polenta, bread with a drizzle of olive oil, garlic and herbs, and a drop or two of red wine, are some of the mainstays of the Mediterranean diet.

colours of the rainbow

One way to maximise your intake of protective food components is to fill your diet with plenty of richly-pigmented plant foods (see *antioxidant colour code*, page 9). Start with vibrant, multi-coloured fruits and vegetables, and herbs and spices: not only do you reap the rewards of antioxidants and phytochemicals that offer long-term protection from lifestyle diseases, such as heart disease and cancer, but you also ensure that your skin, hair, eyes and nails are at their best. You'll gain such benefits as collagen-firming vitamin C and vision-enhancing components, such as lutein, from kiwifruit.

antioxidant colour code

Your guide to antioxidants in fruit, vegetables and other foods

which antioxidant?	colours	which foods?
anthocyanins	red, blue	blueberries, cranberries, raspberries, dark grapes
beta-carotene	orange	carrots, mangoes, apricots
catechins	tawny, red	cocoa, chocolate, red wine, green tea
cryptoxanthins	orange	mangoes, red capsicum, pumpkins
lycopene	red	tomatoes, watermelons, guavas, strawberries, pink grapefruits
lutein	yellow, green	spinach, corn, gold kiwifruit
flavonoids	various	tea, green tea, citrus fruits, apples
phenolic acid	various	apples, citrus fruits, oats
polyphenols	green, red	thyme, oregano, rosemary, ginger, red wine
vitamin C	various	oranges, mangoes, kiwifruit, strawberries, blackcurrants

did you know?

There's no debate about the power of plant foods. In order to help counteract cellular damage from today's lifestyles we know a diet rich in antioxidants is needed. Plant foods contain a huge range of special protective components called phytochemicals, which act as antioxidants to protect different cells of your body.

how much fat should you be getting?

eat less, live longer?

Scientists in the US are conducting laboratory research on the effects of kilojoule, or calorie, restriction (CR). CR appears to slow the metabolic rate and, thus, may slow the rate of ageing. It appears that a fast metabolism may lead to greater damage to the tissues as free radicals are also formed at a greater rate. It is thought that, by slowing your metabolism or, in essence, your "rate of living", you're also slowing the damage that leads to premature ageing and disease progression. This may sound like a good way to stave off old age, however, available human data is scant and inconclusive. There's also a strong argument that we need to uncover a total lifestyle approach that promotes longevity, as it may be possible to achieve results similar to that reported from CR in far less extreme circumstances. It is a well-established fact that a healthy weight range means fewer health problems than being overweight, and the same goes for being underweight.

A key dietary guideline for everyone is to limit saturated fat and moderate total fat intake. The National Health and Medical Research Council (NHMRC) recently launched new guidelines on fat intake. There is no actual recommended dietary intake (RDI) for total fat, but it's advised that you limit your total fat intake to within the range of 20-35 per cent of your recommended kilojoule intake. This differs from person to person, so we've given you some approximate figures based on 30 per cent of kilojoule intake as total fat (see *how much fat?*, page 11). By reading food labels to see how much fat is in different foods, you'll see that some high-fat foods, such as chocolate, burgers and fries, can easily eat into your daily tally. The last column on the fat table shows guidelines on saturated and trans fat intake, which is worked out at 10 per cent of your total kilojoule intake. Again, checking the nutrition information panel on food labels will help you see how some foods, such as butter and processed meats, are very high in saturated fats.

There are also guidelines now emerging on a healthy intake of the different types of polyunsaturated fats. According to the NHMRC, an adequate intake of omega-3 fat should be 160mg/day for men and 90mg/day for women. It's a lot harder to monitor your intake of these fats, as food labels often do not list the different amounts. The best approach is to focus on including more omega-3 fatty acids in your diet and you'll improve your omega-6 to omega-3 ratio at the same time.

the facts on fat

Saturated fat is usually solid at room temperature and is mainly found in animal foods such as processed and fatty meats, and dairy foods such as milk, cheese and butter. It is also found in some plant foods, including coconut and palm oil. Saturated fat is most often used in the manufacture of commercial foods, such as cakes, biscuits, confectionery, takeaway food, etc. It is the type of fat that raises blood cholesterol and increases the risk of cardiovascular disease.

Polyunsaturated fat is mainly found in plant foods, including sunflower, soy bean and safflower oils, and nuts and seeds. It is also found in oily fish, such as salmon, tuna and sardines. Omega-3 and omega-6 fatty acids are types of polyunsaturated fats; omega-3 fats are mainly found in fish and omega-6 fats are mainly found in vegetable oils. Polyunsaturated fats are liquid at room temperature, and can help lower blood cholesterol and reduce the risk of cardiovascular disease.

Monounsaturated fat is found in oils including canola and olive oils, and other plant foods including avocados, nuts and seeds, as well as in lean meat. Monounsaturated fats are generally liquid at room temperature, but may solidify in cold temperatures. These fats can also help lower blood cholesterol and reduce the risk of cardiovascular disease.

Trans fat is found mainly in deep-fried fast foods and processed foods made with shortening and some margarines. It's used by food manufacturers to get the right consistency in foods such as cakes and pastries. Trans fat increases the level of "bad" LDL cholesterol (see panel, right) in much the same way as saturated fat. And worse, it seems to also lower the concentration of "good" HDL cholesterol that's protective against heart disease.

Cholesterol is only found in animal foods – not in plants. It is a fatty substance that is an important part of all animals, including humans. Our bodies produce it naturally, even if we don't eat it. Cholesterol is a problem when there is too much in our blood. Eating too much saturated fat can cause high blood cholesterol.

Sterols occur naturally in all plants. Plant sterols work by blocking the absorption of cholesterol, leading to reduced levels of cholesterol in the blood. They have been shown to lower blood cholesterol levels by an average of 10 per cent, depending on how much is consumed. The concentration of sterols in plants is quite low, and they do not provide a sufficient amount to lower cholesterol absorption, however, recent advances in manufacturing have enabled them to be added in larger amounts to foods such as margarine.

how much fat?

Your guide to your recommended fat intake per day

what group are you?	recommended total fat intake	recommended total daily saturated & trans fat intake
low kilojoule intake (6000kJ/day) young children inactive/elderly	50g	less than 13g
moderate kilojoule intake (8000kJ/day) older children many women inactive men	65g	less than 18g
high kilojoule intake (10,000kJ/day) active teenagers/active men very active women lactating women	80g	less than 22g
very high kilojoule intake (12,000kJ/day) very active teenagers very active men	95g	less than 26g

HDL or LDL, which is better?

HDL (high-density lipoprotein) cholesterol, is often labelled "good" cholesterol because it reduces the amount of LDL, or "bad" cholesterol, in the arteries. The higher the HDL level, the lower the risk of heart disease. When too much LDL (low-density lipoprotein) cholesterol circulates in the blood, it can slowly build up in the walls of the arteries that feed the heart and brain. Together with other substances it can form plaque, a thick, hard deposit that can clog the arteries. This condition is known as atherosclerosis, and can cause a heart attack or stroke.

overweight or obese?

Fat is deposited in our bodies when the kilojoules (energy) we consume is greater than the kilojoules we use up. Small imbalances over long periods of time can cause you to become overweight or obese. Obesity rates in Australia have more than doubled over the past 20 years. Around seven million Australians are now overweight or obese, and it is estimated that, at the current rate of increase, about 75 per cent of the Australian population will be overweight or obese by 2020.

Overweight and obesity are defined by the World Health Organization using the body mass index (BMI), which is calculated by dividing a person's weight in kilograms by their height in metres squared. For example, a person who is 1.65m tall and weighs 64kg would have a BMI of 24. People with a BMI of 25-29 are classified as overweight, while those with a BMI of 30 or greater are classified as obese. There are a number of BMI calculators on the internet if you want to work out your BMI.

drink to your health

We all know that to maintain optimal wellbeing we need to balance all aspects of our diet, including what we drink. Water is the natural choice to keep body organs and cells hydrated, with eight glasses for women and 10 glasses for men widely accepted as optimal. There are other beverages, however, but can they help keep you hydrated?

sounds juicy

Juicing has always been caught up in the dieting cycle, falling in and out of popularity over time. Juices can be tangy, refreshing and a great way to keep up your daily fluid tally. As they contain a concentrated source of fruit or vegetables, they can also act as a vitamin boost if your diet is not as balanced as it should be. Juices are a healthier alternative to soft drinks as they provide valuable nutrients rather than empty kilojoules. And a daily juice can be a good way of helping reach your fruit/vegetable target of 2-5 servings. Just remember, though, you generally fall short on fibre as it's mainly contained in the skin and pulp left behind.

happy hour

One benefit of alcohol, particularly red wine, has been linked to a healthy heart. Red wine contains potent antioxidants known as polyphenols that offer many cardio-protective properties, which may be one reason that the French, known to be great drinkers of red wine, can have diets traditionally high in saturated fats yet also have low rates of heart disease.

Red wine has also been linked with reduced risks of lung and prostate cancer, although the data is still emerging and not yet conclusive. One study on lung cancer risk showed positive benefits from moderate red wine consumption, but not with white wine, while a separate study showed that consuming a glass of red wine every day may halve a man's risk of prostate cancer.

caffeine culture

Caffeine is the most widely used drug worldwide, with the most common sources being coffee, tea, cola soft drinks, chocolate and energy drinks. In Australia, caffeine consumption from coffee and tea is estimated at 232mg per adult/day (with 87 per cent of the caffeine being supplied by coffee). This amount of caffeine would be supplied by around three cups of coffee or around seven cups of tea. However, research reports that only 61 per cent of adults drink coffee, therefore, to reach this national average of 232mg/day, many coffee drinkers would easily consume at least five or six cups of coffee a day.

how much is too much juice?

Being a concentrated source of fruit and vegetables also means that juices are generally a concentrated source of kilojoules. If trying to lose weight, it's best to stick to water and teas for your main beverages, and sugar-free or diet soft drink when you feel like something sweet, as they have virtually no kilojoules; count juices as part of your daily food intake.

how much is too much alcohol?

Overall, drinking small amounts (1-2 standard servings) appears to offer health benefits. However, researchers are careful to add that alcohol affects people in different ways, and consumption patterns are very important, as heavy or binge drinking poses many serious health risks. Before you toast to good health every night, it's also worth keeping in mind that wine, or any alcohol for that matter, is high in kilojoules, and must be factored into your weight-loss plan.

how much is too much caffeine?

From a health perspective the recommended intake of caffeine is less than 250-300mg/day (that's just three average cups of coffee). Enjoy the caffeine culture, but be sure to drink other fluids as well.

foods that fight type-2 diabetes

Diabetes is a condition characterised by high blood-sugar levels. There are two main types of diabetes – Type 1 or insulin-dependant diabetes where the pancreas does not produce enough insulin, and Type 2 diabetes (previously known as non-insulin dependant diabetes or mature-onset diabetes) where the insulin produced is not strong enough to control the level of sugar in the blood. People with Type 2 diabetes are often overweight and, in simple terms, excess body fat blocks the action of insulin so it does not work efficiently at lowering blood-sugar levels. With the growing obesity problem, it's no surprise to hear that 1.2 million people have Type 2 diabetes and a further 2 million have a condition known as insulin resistance or pre-diabetes.

eat for health

The principles of dietary prevention of diabetes include achieving a healthy weight with a diet low to moderate in fat (particularly saturated fat), the right types of carbohydrates and, as always, regular physical activity. Regular meals and snacks are also important.

For many years, people with diabetes cut sugar from their diets, restricted their intake of starchy foods and ate as much fat as they liked, and the result was that they ended up in coronary care wards. Today, dietitians believe that healthy eating for diabetes should be no different than for anyone else. The key issue for treatment is the same as for protection, and that is to maintain a healthy weight, do plenty of physical activity (including strength training) and follow a low-saturated fat, high-fibre diet that includes wholegrains, fruit and vegetables. Studies have shown that people who eat 2-3 servings of wholegrain foods each day are 20-30 per cent less likely to develop Type 2 diabetes than people who don't eat any.

what is GI?

The glycaemic index (GI) is simply the rate at which a carbohydrate-rich food converts to sugar (or glucose) in the bloodstream. Carbohydrate foods that are broken down quickly during digestion, causing a rapid rise in blood sugar levels, are known as high-GI foods. On the other hand, carbohydrates that break down more slowly during digestion, causing a slower and steadier rise in blood sugar, are known as low-GI foods.

For people with existing or pre-diabetes, the preferred carbohydrates are the low-GI foods. Research has shown that blood-sugar levels are more easily controlled when more low-GI foods are included in the diet. A good guide is to aim to have a least one low-GI food per meal or snack.

your health check

Risk factors for diabetes include being overweight or obese, high blood pressure, a family history, gestational diabetes in pregnancy, polycystic ovary syndrome and heart disease. The risk of diabetes also increases with age, and anyone over the age of 55 years should discuss having a blood glucose tolerance test with their GP. It's estimated that half the people with diabetes do not know they have it and are missing out on effective dietary and medical management.

fighting foods checklist

Low-GI foods include:

- Wholegrain breads, including fruit loaf and soy and linseed bread
- Breakfast cereals, including oats, porridge and bran
- Pasta and noodles
- All legumes, including baked beans
- Basmati or doongara rice
- Orchard fruits, including apples, oranges, peaches and pears
- Sweet corn and sweet potato
- Reduced-fat yogurt and milk

fighting foods news flash

It seems that people with diabetes should be going nuts. Researchers at the University of Wollongong have shown that the "good oils" in walnuts can help with the management of Type 2 diabetes. Research demonstrated that a diet including 8-10 walnuts a day delivered the right kinds of fats and fatty acids that might help the body with insulin resistance, which can be a major problem.

foods that fight bowel disorders

fighting foods checklist

- Fruit and vegetables
- Wholegrain breads, pasta, rice and cereals
- All legumes, including baked beans
- Nuts and seeds
- Probiotic yogurts and drinks
- Foods enriched with inulin or resistant starch like hi-maize, known as "invisible fibre" (see *don't forget the fibre*, page 7)
- Plenty of fluids (8-10 glasses of water a day)

fabulous fibre

A high-fibre diet, between 30-50g of total dietary fibre a day, is recommended for prevention of many common bowel disorders including diverticulitis (small pocket-like sacs in the lining of the colon), constipation and haemorrhoids. Fibre helps soften your stools (faeces) and makes waste products pass more quickly through your system. This helps decrease the pressure build-up in your bowels and prevents straining and damage to the bowel lining.

There are many conditions and diseases, from constipation to colon cancer, that can affect your bowel. Chances are at some stage in your life you will experience a bowel condition and, even though it may not be life threatening, bowel disorders can certainly disrupt your daily life and wellbeing. The good news is that there is a lot of scientific knowledge on how to keep your bowel healthy through the right diet and lifestyle. This section focuses on promoting bowel health and, using a common condition, irritable bowel syndrome (IBS), shows how complex healthy bowel management can be.

your health check

Bowel function varies greatly from individual to individual and, to a lesser extent, within individuals from day to day. It's not just the food you eat that affects your bowels. Stress, medications, travel and alcohol are a few of the other things that can cause changes to regular bowel habits.

The best indication of a well-functioning bowel is regularity – whether for you that means twice a day or once every two days – with easy to pass, well-formed stools (bowel motions). If your usual pattern changes drastically for no apparent cause, or because of a suspected bout of food poisoning, or you have the presence of blood or mucus in your stools, see your doctor. It's important to note that persistent constipation can be as great a concern as persistent diarrhoea.

Routine colonoscopies are recommended for people with a family history of colon cancer, as early detection is the key to successful treatment. Blood tests can pick up anaemia due to suspected bleeding in the gut, and stool studies can detect infection and strains of bad bacteria. Breath tests are now also used to diagnose peptic ulcers and types of food malabsorption, like fructose (fruit sugar) malabsorption experienced by some people with irritable bowel syndrome.

eat for health

The principles of dietary prevention of bowel disorders include following a healthy diet high in fibre and low in fat and salt, with sufficient fluid intake to maintain hydration and lubricate waste in the bowels. Regular intake of foods with probiotics (see *fighting foods news flash*, page 15) can help promote an optimal balance of good bacteria that offer superior protection. Your overall focus, as with other lifestyle diseases, should be on maintaining a healthy weight through the right diet and regular physical activity, plus working at maximising your wellbeing by using effective stress management and cutting out unhealthy habits like smoking and excessive alcohol consumption.

which treatment is right for you?

Unlike prevention, dietary treatment for bowel disease is very specialised, and differs greatly from condition to condition. What works for ulcerative colitis is not what works for lactose intolerance. And what works for one person with irritable bowel syndrome is not guaranteed to work for the next. That's why expert care under a gastroenterologist is vital, and consultation with an accredited practising dietitian (APD) is needed to find the right diet for you.

Take irritable bowel syndrome, or IBS, as an example. This functional disorder of the gut affects approximately 15-30 per cent of all Australians. IBS describes a collection of symptoms including abdominal pain, diarrhoea, gas (wind), varying bowel habit, bloating or urgency to empty the bowel. Symptoms vary from person to person, and can vary from chronic attacks lasting weeks to mild discomfort over a few hours. The cause of IBS is unknown, and there is no standard treatment as individual responses are so varied. As IBS does not reduce life expectancy, many people in the past were given limited advice and treatment options and simply told to "live with it". However, these days, due to IBS being recognised as very costly to the community in terms of money spent on medical consultations and missed days of work, the condition is the focus of much new research.

As IBS is incredibly complex, dietary therapy must be individualised. Some people may be sensitive to certain foods and can identify these as triggers. Researchers are also looking at fructose malabsorption in some people with IBS. Fructose is a naturally occurring sugar found in many fruits, some vegetables and honey. As with lactose (milk sugar) intolerance, it appears that not everyone has the ability to absorb fructose properly. When fructose is not fully digested, it is passed from the digestive tract to the colon where the gut bacteria use the fructose as a food source. In the process, hydrogen gas is produced, and symptoms of bloating, cramps and diarrhoea may be experienced.

Fructose malabsorption can be diagnosed via hydrogen breath tests and a low-fructose diet is prescribed. Unfortunately, the diet is not as simple as just monitoring your fruit intake, as many commercial foods use a type of fructose as their sweetener. Also, fruits differ in their fructose content and their fructose to glucose ratio, which determines the extent of malabsorption. Generally, people with fructose malabsorption can still enjoy certain fruits and get the minimum two servings a day recommended for all adults. Not everyone with IBS has fructose malabsorption, and that's why individual medical care and expert dietary advice is needed for effective treatment and management of all major bowel disorders.

fighting foods news flash

Probiotics are the good bacteria that can help keep your gut in top working order. With the help of probiotics your system is more likely to cope when any unwanted gatecrashers arrive, like that bout of Bali belly or childhood rotavirus (a type of gastroenteritis), and you're also more likely to escape any diarrhoea side effects during a course of antibiotics.

Probiotics have also been shown to help with immune function especially in children and the elderly, and can help treat gastric ulcers. In essence, probiotics strengthen the immune defence at the gut wall, stopping disease-causing bugs from getting in and causing health problems.

The latest research is showing very promising studies on the effect of probiotics on certain types of cancer, particularly bowel cancer, where powerful bacteria are working to protect bowel cells. And there is evidence that probiotics may also be beneficial in bladder and breast cancer.

In order to get maximum benefit from probiotics you need to be getting sufficient quantities every day. Research indicates that you need to consume 100 million live bacteria or more every day. A daily probiotic drink, or 200g of probiotic yogurt, should provide you with the right amount.

foods that fight cancer

fighting foods checklist

- Dark leafy greens
- Yellow/orange vegetables and fruits
- Garlic, onions, chives and leeks
- Brussels sprouts, broccoli, cabbage and cauliflower
- Citrus fruits, melon, kiwifruit and berries
- Tomatoes
- Wholegrains, nuts and seeds
- Legumes
- Herbs and spices (mint, basil, oregano, sage, thyme, rosemary, parsley, linseed, ginger, turmeric, dill, coriander, fennel, cumin, anise and caraway; see *culinary herbs*, page 17)

Diet-related cancers in Australia account for the loss of more than 7000 potential years of life. Between 30 and 40 per cent of cancers are diet-related, including bowel, breast and stomach cancer. Bowel cancer affects approximately 9500 Australians and kills around 3500 every year, and breast cancer is the most common cause of cancer death in women.

your health check

Recent research suggests that a modifiable risk factor, including obesity, low fruit and vegetable intake, physical inactivity, smoking and alcohol use, may be a contributing factor in more than a third of cancers.

There is now strong evidence that obesity is a risk factor for some cancers, such as bowel, prostate, postmenopausal breast, uterine and renal (kidney) cell cancer. There are many possible reasons and the exact mechanisms are unclear, however, it is thought one link may be that being overweight or physically inactive cause the body to secrete higher amounts of insulin and growth factors. This, in turn, can cause fast growth and genetic changes to body cells and increases the risk of stimulating cancer-causing cells.

eat to beat

We have known for some time that reducing your dietary intake of saturated fat, eating more plant foods rich in dietary fibre and phytochemicals, maintaining a healthy body weight and drinking alcohol in moderation are important considerations in cancer prevention. A diet rich in grains, fruit and vegetables is particularly important. Not only are these foods low in saturated fat and high in fibre, they also contain antioxidants, which help to fight cancer. These antioxidants work to clean up the free radicals, or unstable molecules, in your body that can cause cellular changes that may lead to cancer.

Antioxidants are still big news, but it seems not all antioxidants are equal. Some research found it difficult to separate the benefit of the antioxidant from the other healthy parts of the diet. It seems antioxidants may work best in natural foods, and there may be a cooperation between other antioxidants and phytochemicals in the food, which creates the greatest benefit.

The Cancer Council Australia recommends eating meat in moderation: 3-4 servings of cooked lean red meat each week and limiting processed meats. You should also limit high heat forms of cooking meat, such as using the barbecue, as the smoking and charring of meat may also cause the production of harmful chemicals. Whether or not these chemicals cause cancer in humans has not been categorically proven, however, animal studies reveal some concerns.

drink for health

The Cancer Council Australia also recommends you limit or avoid drinking alcohol. Their guidelines are to have one or two alcohol-free days a week, and limit yourself on other days to no more than one standard drink for women and two standard drinks for men.

eat for health

There is no eating plan to cure cancer, but rather a focus on good nutrition to boost your immunity and help your body cope with treatment and repair of body tissues. If you've been diagnosed with cancer, it's likely that eating problems may occur, especially during treatment. Side effects vary with the type of cancer and treatment, however, they may include nausea and loss of appetite, sore mouth and throat, loss of taste, and constipation or diarrhoea.

To help manage these symptoms you may need to make changes to your usual diet, such as having small, frequent meals and including energy supplement drinks. Your doctor and dietitian will advise you on the best personal plan.

It's also important to remember there are many unproven dietary treatments for cancer. These include mega doses of vitamins, herbal supplements, macrobiotic diets (from which all meat and dairy, several kinds of fruit and vegetables and processed food, among other things, are banned) and juice therapies, which claim to strengthen the body's immunity and fight cancer cells. The Cancer Council Australia advises there is little evidence to support these treatments, and high levels of many vitamins and herbal compounds can be poisonous and may interfere with chemotherapy. Always talk to your doctor before taking supplements and exploring other dietary therapies.

culinary herbs

As herbs are consumed in relatively small servings compared to many other plant foods, it is, in some ways, unfair to compare their nutrient content on a per serving basis. For example, even though many herbs are high in vitamin C, you're not going to get anywhere close to your daily needs with, say, a parsley garnish on a bowl of soup. Unless you're into eating a bowl of tabbouleh every day, getting your vitamin C allowance from eating an orange or kiwifruit seems so much easier.

However, when you dig a little deeper and look at the phytochemicals in herbs, the grass may turn out to be a little greener. It seems that studies of culinary herbs show that they may have higher levels of antioxidant capacity than medicinal herbs or fruits and vegetables. Furthermore, adding antioxidant-rich herbs to other foods, like oregano to a tomato salad, may enhance the overall antioxidant capacity of the carrier foods, i.e., the main food in the meal. Using herbs also reduces the need to use salt as a flavouring, which can be helpful in managing high blood pressure.

fighting foods news flash

Recent research suggests that vitamin D and diets rich in carotenoids (beta-carotene, lutein, cryptoxanthin and lycopene) may protect against skin cancers and reduce melanoma (skin cancer) risk. It appears that carotenoids filter harmful rays in sunlight that can damage human cells.

what is a standard drink?

A standard drink contains 10g of alcohol: this is equal to one glass of full strength beer (285ml) or two 285ml glasses of light beer. It is also equal to one small (100ml) glass of wine, one measure (30ml) of spirits or one small glass (60ml) of fortified wine such as sherry or port.

did you know?

Cancer is the name for diseases in which the body's cells become abnormal and divide without control. These cells then invade healthy tissues, affecting their ability to function normally. According to The Cancer Council Australia, more than 88,000 new cases of cancer are diagnosed each year in Australia; the most common cancers are bowel, breast, prostate, melanoma (skin) and lung cancer. The survival rate for many common cancers has increased by more than 30 per cent and, these days, more than half the cancer cases are successfully treated.

fighting foods checklist

- Dairy products: milk, cheese and yogurt (including low-fat varieties)
- Canned fish with edible bones, such as salmon and sardines
- Nuts and seeds
- Green leafy vegetables and asian greens
- Tofu and other soy alternatives
- Calcium-fortified soy drinks and other calcium-fortified foods

fighting foods news flash

The other nutrient important for strong bones is vitamin D, which is used to help the body absorb calcium. These days, many people are not getting enough vitamin D and are at a greater risk of falls and fractures. As vitamin D is found in only small quantities in few foods – egg yolks, liver, oily fish (salmon, herring, mackerel, sardines and trout) and fortified dairy products and margarines – most people are unlikely to meet their requirements through diet alone. The best source of vitamin D is sunlight, so try to get a little outdoor exercise each day. People with limited opportunity for sun exposure would benefit from vitamin D-fortified foods, such as margarines and dairy products. There is a call for more vitamin D fortification of foods especially for children and adolescents.

foods that fight osteoporosis

Breaking a hip or shrinking in height used to be simply accepted as just part of ageing, but we now know better. Osteoporosis is a condition in which bones lose calcium, become fragile and fracture more readily. It affects one in every 10 Australians, causing an osteoporotic fracture in one in two women and one in three men over the age of 60.

your health check

Risk factors for osteoporosis include a family history, poor calcium intake, lack of vitamin D, low exercise levels, smoking, high alcohol and salt intake, and possibly high caffeine intakes, delayed menarche (onset of menstruation), early menopause (cessation of menstruation) and some medications.

Prevention of osteoporosis is a life-long commitment. Building strong bones, especially before the age of 35, is one of the best defences against developing osteoporosis. It appears that childhood and adolescence is not only an important time for growing bones, but also an important time for determining bone density. By the age of 20, 90-95 per cent of peak bone mass is attained. Once we reach our mid 30s our peak bone mass starts to decline. Decreasing levels of oestrogen during menopause further accelerates bone loss. However, while it is best to build healthy bones early through the right diet and physical weight-bearing activity, it's never too late to start taking care of your bones.

the importance of calcium

The key to healthy bone habits is to ensure you're getting your daily requirements of bone-building nutrients like protein and calcium. Most Australians eat enough protein, but it's the calcium that some may be missing.

Adults need 1000mg calcium each day (roughly 3-4 dairy servings), with an additional 300mg during pregnancy, breastfeeding, menopause and adolescent growth spurts. Dairy products are an excellent source of calcium as they are convenient, offer many other important nutrients such as protein, and the calcium is readily absorbable.

The Australian Dietary Guidelines now recommend reduced-fat dairy products for most people over the age of 2 years, as they contain less saturated fat and have higher amounts of calcium. If you are lactose intolerant, vegan or don't like dairy products, there are many other good sources of calcium available, such as fortified soy products, green leafy vegetables, nuts and the edible bones in fish. However, it's important to note that we don't absorb the calcium as well from plant sources.

eat for health

Too much salt (sodium), caffeine and alcohol are associated with decreased bone density and increased risk of bone fractures. Too much sodium in the diet can cause calcium to be excreted from the body, so it's important to choose low-salt foods to help protect your bones.

Foods containing phytates (wholegrain cereals, seeds, soy and legumes) or oxalates (tea, spinach and rhubarb) can also bind calcium, making it unavailable for absorption. While some of these foods also contain calcium, it is not absorbed as efficiently as other foods, such as dairy. For example, about 5 per cent of the calcium in spinach is absorbed compared to about 30 per cent of the calcium in milk.

calcium counter

which food?	what's a serving?	how much calcium (mg)?
almonds	25	70
breakfast cereal, fortified	1 cup	187
broccoli, boiled	1 piece	15
cheese, cheddar	30g	232
cheese, cheddar, reduced-fat	30g	241
cheese, cheddar, low-fat	30g	313
cheese, cottage, low-fat	½ cup	89
cheese, ricotta	½ cup	293
chocolate	30g	75
fish, uncoated, steamed	150g	39
ice-cream	1 scoop	53
milk, regular	250ml	294
milk, reduced-fat	250ml	353
milk, skim	250ml	319
milk, soy, fortified	250ml	302
milk, soy, low-fat	250ml	286
milk, soy, unfortified	250ml	34
peanuts, raw	25	11
prawns, king, boiled	5 average	108
rhubarb, stewed	1 cup	40
salmon, canned, with bones	100g	335
sardines, canned in oil/brine	5	285
sesame seeds	1 tablespoon (20g)	12
spinach, boiled	1 cup	73
tofu, cooked	100g	330
tuna, canned in brine	100g	8
yogurt, regular	200g	340
yogurt, reduced-fat	200g	310
yogurt, low-fat/fat-free, fruit	200g	360
yogurt, low-fat/fat-free, plain	200g	420
yogurt drink, reduced-fat	200g	336
yogurt, frozen, soft serve, regular	200g	338
yogurt, frozen, soft serve, reduced-fat	200g	362

get plenty of exercise

Exercise helps to keep bones strong and reduces the chance of injury. Weight-bearing exercises, such as jumping, skipping, walking, aerobics or netball, and strength-training exercises, such as pump (non-impact weight training) or circuit (continuous cardiovascular workout) classes are the best exercises for strong bones. It is good to do a variety of exercises so that stress is placed on a variety of bones and muscles, for example, tennis players have more bone strength in their dominant arm.

caffeine versus calcium

There has been speculation that caffeine increases the risk of osteoporosis. It's true that it increases calcium excretion, but there is debate as to whether this adversely affects bone health.

foods that fight cardiovascular disease

fighting foods checklist

- Fish: salmon, sardines, tuna, mackerel, ocean trout
- Omega-3 rich oils: canola, linseed, walnut, soybean and wheat germ
- Oats, oat bran, muesli, barley
- Monounsaturated oils and fats: olive and canola oils and margarines
- Brightly coloured fruits and vegetables
- Rice bran, brown rice and other wholegrain cereals
- Nuts: walnuts, almonds
- Avocado
- Legumes
- Garlic

fighting foods news flash

Although scientists have known for a long time that olive is the good oil when it comes to lowering cholesterol levels, exciting new research is uncovering other heart benefits. It appears that the phenolic compounds (a type of antioxidant) in olive oil also have anti-inflammatory and anti-clotting factors that improve the health of blood vessels. In one study, those who ate olive oil had improved blood flow after the meal; this was compared with similar studies showing that high-fat meals, such as hamburgers and chips, impaired blood vessel function. Researchers recommend that virgin or extra virgin olive oil may be best, as these oils do not undergo much processing and, therefore, retain more antioxidants.

Heart disease is still the major killer in our society, taking more lives than breast and lung cancer combined. In fact, cardiovascular disease (which affects the heart and blood vessels) affects one in six Australians (over 3.2 million people) and one Australian dies from this condition every 10 minutes. Many believe that women have a decreased risk of heart disease compared with men. However, while this is true for young women because the hormone oestrogen offers some protection, after menopause the risk of heart disease is trebled for women, placing them at the same risk as men.

your health check

There are many risk factors associated with heart disease – family history, high blood pressure, high blood-fats such as cholesterol and triglycerides, diabetes, smoking, obesity, physical inactivity and inability to cope with stress. Some of these we have no control over, such as our choice of parents or whether we're male or female, but we do have control over many of the other risk factors, and we can also make big heart-friendly changes to our diet.

eat for health

The principles of dietary prevention and management of heart disease are basically the same. The first step should be to achieve and maintain a healthy weight, with focus on losing central body fat distribution. Aim for a waist circumference of less than 94cm in men and less than 80cm for women.

The next focus is on managing healthy blood-fat levels. Your overall diet should be low in saturated fat, found in foods like biscuits, cakes, butter, cream and fatty and processed meats. For a helping hand to lower LDL or "bad" cholesterol, switch from butter to a poly or monounsaturated table spread or, better still, try a plant sterol margarine (see *the latest and greatest*, page 24, for more information), or go Mediterranean-style and drizzle a little olive oil on crusty bread.

You should also increase your soluble fibre intake from wholegrains such as oats and legumes (lentils, chickpeas and beans) plus fruit and vegetables, monitor your alcohol intake and eat oily fish (salmon, tuna, sardines, mackerel, gemfish, mullet and herring) with heart-friendly omega-3s at least twice a week.

foods that fight arthritis

The key issue with diet and arthritis is not to fall victim to fads and fallacies. The most common myth is to cut out foods such as citrus fruits, tomatoes, eggplant and red capscium in the belief that these "acidic" foods will increase inflammation and pain. The research is scant and, even though some people may feel better from eliminating certain foods from their diet, there is not enough scientific justification to do so. In fact, low vitamin C levels can increase the risk of developing inflammatory (rheumatoid) arthritis, so it's better to increase your intake of fruits and vegetables rather than the other way around. One fruit that scientists believe may bring osteoarthritis to its knees is the pomegranate, which may decrease inflammation and slow down the enzymes that erode cartilage (see *the latest and greatest*, page 24, for more information).

There has been considerable research into omega-3 fatty acids and the impact they have on reducing inflammation in the joints, and the news is good. If you have arthritis, eat plenty of omega-3 rich oily fish at least twice a week. As well, make sure you're are not overweight, as excess weight can put stress and strain on the joints.

Some people may experience anti-inflammatory benefits from supplements such as green-lipped mussel extract, glucosamine and fish oil but, as always, it is best to discuss the use of supplements with your doctor.

foods that fight menopause symptoms

Menopause is a natural event that is said to have occurred when a woman has not menstruated naturally for 12 consecutive months. It usually occurs between the ages of 45 and 55. During menopause, many women may experience a number of symptoms including hot flushes and night sweats, aches and pains, headaches, tiredness, irritability, depression, crawling or itching sensations under the skin, vaginal dryness, reduced libido (sex drive), urinary frequency, low self-esteem, sleeping difficulty and forgetfulness.

Soy foods contain a type of phytoestrogen known as isoflavones, and they have been reported to be beneficial to some women during menopause, however, dietary phytoestrogens are much weaker than the oestrogen produced naturally in the body or gained through hormone replacement therapy. Studies mostly indicate that increased consumption of phytoestrogens by postmenopausal women is no more effective than a placebo in reducing hot flushes.

The main scientific support for a diet high in phytoestrogens is in helping maintain heart health. Good sources of phytoestrogens include soy and linseed bread, soy beans, tofu, wholegrains and legumes. A high-soy diet has been shown to lower LDL "bad" cholesterol and improve blood vessel function, and there is favourable research on breast and uterine cancer and osteoporosis prevention.

Oestrogen, a hormone important for maintaining healthy bones, decreases during menopause, which causes the bones to lose calcium and other minerals at a much faster rate than they did before, therefore, postmenopausal women are more prone to health problems such as osteoporosis. A diet rich in calcium and vitamin D (see *fighting foods checklist*, page 18) and plenty of weight-bearing exercise, is important to maintain good bone health.

did you know?

Arthritis is the inflammation of a joint(s) causing pain, swelling and stiffness. It's a debilitating disease and is Australia's major cause of disability and pain. According to Arthritis Australia, one in six Australians has arthritis, and it isn't just a part of getting older; most people diagnosed with arthritis are of working age, and children also can get arthritis (known as juvenile arthritis).

There are more than 120 different types of arthritis, and most forms are thought to be a reaction of the body against its own joint tissues (known as an autoimmune disease); gout, osteoarthritis, rheumatoid arthritis, and lupus are some of the most common forms of arthritis. There's no cure, but you've got to "move it or lose it", as rest can make pain and other symptoms much worse.

fighting foods checklist

- High-calcium, low-fat dairy foods
- Foods high in phytoestrogens, such as soy beans, tofu and other soy alternatives
- Fresh vegetables, fruits, cereals and whole grains
- Drink 8 glasses of water daily
- Decrease intake of caffeine (coffee, tea, cola, chocolate)
- Limit alcohol to one to two standard glasses, or less, per day

hero foods the ones that fight for your life

Another approach to eating for longevity is to simply fill your plate with plenty of hero foods everyday. Researchers have expanded this concept into the idea of the perfect meal, called the "polymeal". Their research has found that, in theory, if someone aged over 50 has the daily equivalent of the polymeal, they reduce their chances of getting heart disease by around 76 per cent. For men this translates to living 6.6 years longer and for women 4.8 years longer.

This meal includes 400g of fruit and vegetables, 150ml of wine, 100g of dark chocolate, 2.7g (a clove or two) of garlic, 68g (a handful or so) of almonds and 114g of fish, consumed four times a week.

So, what else should you be putting on your plate? Here are some of the hero foods that are important for good health.

Blueberries These brightly coloured fruits deliver high levels of antioxidants called anthocyanins. Anthocyanins have been shown to lower cholesterol, prevent blood clotting, protect body cells and decrease the effects of brain ageing. That's why they're sometimes referred to as "brainberries".

Broccoli and broccolini These belong to the brassica family and are packed with nutrients like vitamins C and A, riboflavin, folate, calcium and iron. They also contain indoles, shown to block oestrogen receptors in breast cancer cells, and sulforaphane, which also kills abnormal cells.

Chilli We all envy people with a speedy metabolism, those who can eat what they like without gaining weight. If only there was an internal switch that would allow us all to rev up our metabolism as needed. Probably the best way of boosting your metabolism is keeping physically active, but there's also evidence that chilli may fire things up, too. Chilli contains a compound called capsaicin, responsible for its super hot status, which is thought to temporarily boost metabolism.

Citrus fruits A CSIRO report shows a compelling trend of protection against various types of cancers from eating citrus fruits such as oranges, lemons, limes and grapefruit. The greatest protection is for cancers of the mouth, oesophagus, larynx and stomach, where studies showed risk reductions of 40-50 per cent by consuming 1-2 servings of citrus fruit a day.

Garlic Allicin, the substance in garlic that gives it the characteristic smell, also inhibits the growth of harmful bacteria and may play a role in enhancing immune function, protecting cells and lowering cholesterol levels. Add fresh garlic to winter soups and stews as well as to stir-fries and pasta sauces for maximum benefit.

Oats Oats are the superstars of the wholegrains. Wholegrain foods are associated with reduced cardiovascular disease and several cancers, with a 68 per cent decreased risk of coronary heart disease observed in high-wholegrain diets. Oats are rich in beta glucan, a soluble fibre, and are low GI. They can help lower LDL "bad" cholesterol, control blood-sugar levels and help with satiety (feelings of fullness). They also contain potent phytochemicals, phenolic compounds in the outer layer of grain, which act as antioxidants.

Probiotic yogurt You get a great calcium boost from yogurt, but it's the probiotics that make it a hero food. Probiotics, sometimes referred to as "aBc" bacteria, are live cultures found in certain yogurt, and there are different types or strains available. Emerging scientific evidence suggests that probiotics offer a host of benefits including promoting gut health, immune protection, reduced risk of some cancers, cholesterol lowering, as well as helping treat conditions like traveller and toddler diarrhoea and atopic eczema (an itchy inflammation of the skin).

Sardines and other oily fish This heart-friendly, omega-3 and zinc-rich fish, makes a perfect grilled lunch, and they're also good news for osteoporosis prevention. Sardines contain edible bones with calcium and significant sources of vitamin D. Sunlight also provides vitamin D to the body, however, dietary vitamin D may be more important as we "slip, slop, slap" to prevent exposure to harmful sunrays.

Soy beans These beans are an excellent source of high-quality protein, containing twice as much protein as any other legume. The active ingredients are the soy protein and plant phytoestrogens (isoflavones), which have positive benefits for heart health and possibly diabetes control, cancer protection (breast, bowel and prostate) and decreasing menopausal symptoms.

Spinach This dark-green leafy vegetable contains a combination of phytonutrients and antioxidants including vitamin K, coenzyme Q10, folate, iron and carotenoids (lutein, zeaxanthin). Folate is especially important for women planning pregnancies, heart health and cancer protection, as well as brain health and the protection of genetic material (DNA). So it's not just Popeye who should be getting his fill.

Tomato These vibrant red fruits are packed with the antioxidant lycopene, which offers a host of benefits including heart health and protection against prostate cancer. Interestingly, the absorption of the lycopene is increased in tomatoes by cooking them in a small amount of olive oil. Great news for pasta lovers.

the latest and greatest

As scientists dig deeper into nutrition research they are constantly uncovering emerging hero foods or new evidence of the power of functional foods. Here's a taste of some of the latest research.

Chocolate (dark) Justifying a chocolate fix has just got a whole lot easier with interesting new research revealing a range of health benefits. So, instead of feeling guilty about your next indulgence, you could treat it as doctor's orders.

Antioxidant discoveries are popping up all over the place, even in chocolate; cocoa extract, used to make chocolate, contains potent antioxidants called flavonoids belonging to the class known as phenolics, with dark chocolate having higher levels than milk chocolate.

Australian researchers have confirmed the antioxidant activity in chocolate. They found that, even at low concentrations, chocolate was able to inhibit and protect body cells from damage by free radicals. In addition, scientists in the US found that a hot cocoa drink had nearly twice the antioxidants of red wine and up to three times those found in green tea.

And further information has cleared up any confusion about chocolate's potential to raise cholesterol levels. The fat in chocolate is predominantly saturated, historically found to raise blood cholesterol levels. However, chocolate contains a unique saturated fatty acid known as stearic acid that does not promote the same cholesterol-raising effect as other saturated fats. Studies have confirmed that diets containing cocoa and chocolate have a neutral effect on blood cholesterol levels and, due to the flavonoid content, a little chocolate may, in fact, turn out to be a positive inclusion in diets for a healthy heart.

Green and gold kiwifruit Kiwifruit is an excellent source of the antioxidant vitamins E and C, folate and polyphenols, and is one of the most nutrient-dense fruits with low kilojoules. Gold kiwifruit has twice the vitamin C of an orange and the same potassium content as a banana. Both green and gold also contain zinc, folate, magnesium and dietary fibre. With very powerful antioxidants, kiwifruit has been studied for its heart, blood vessel and cancer protection, enhanced immunity and protection against macular degeneration (a leading form of blindness).

In a US study, kiwifruit was shown to contain more vitamins and minerals than 27 of the most commonly eaten fruits. And recent research from Norway shows that eating 2-3 kiwifruit a day can thin the blood, reduce blood clotting and decrease the risk of heart disease in healthy individuals.

pomegranates

Nuts Nuts contain healthy oils, fibre, vitamins and minerals, potent phytochemicals and the amino acid arginine (useful in enhancing the immune system). They're no longer a dieter's foe with evidence that nuts, in moderation, won't lead to weight gain. There's also compelling research linking nuts and heart health with findings that a serving of nuts (30-45g), five times a week may cut the risk of coronary heart disease by 20-40 per cent.

Each type of nut has a special makeup, and each are nut heroes in their own way. For example, one brazil nut contains the recommended daily intake of the nutrient selenium, an immune-system booster that also acts in conjunction with other antioxidants to protect body cells. And frequent consumption of macadamias may decrease levels of LDL "bad" cholesterol levels. Try and mix your nuts in order to reap the full benefits.

Plant sterol margarines These are a special class of margarines made with naturally occurring plant components known as plant sterols. The latest research has shown them to be particularly effective in reducing cholesterol absorption.

Trials conducted in Melbourne show that a daily intake of 2-3g of plant sterols can reduce LDL "bad" cholesterol by 10 per cent in three weeks. This translates to 2-3 servings of plant sterol margarine every day, equivalent to the amount you would put on 2-3 slices of bread.

Pomegranates This ancient and exotic fruit is being hailed as a heart protector. Scientists have shown that drinking a daily glass of pomegranate juice can reduce the risk of cardiovascular disease by clearing clogged arteries and may even reverse the progression of the disease.

Claims are that this fruit juice is higher in antioxidants than red wine and green tea. This pomegranate potion may also reduce inflammation in conditions like arthritis, and has the potential to kill prostate cancer cells.

Rosemary Everybody loves a barbie, but in recent times concerns have been raised about the potentially cancer-causing compounds that are formed when meat is grilled at high temperatures – experts believe that the charred, blackened bits on meat contain chemicals called heterocyclic amines, or HCAs, which may be cancer-causing.

However, recent research has revealed there may be more to the perfect flavour match of lamb and rosemary. When meat was rubbed with antioxidant extracts of common herbs like rosemary, basil, oregano and thyme, the levels of harmful compounds were reduced. This effect was thought to be due to the powerful antioxidants in herbs soaking up these HCA free radicals.

foods that fight brain ageing

Considering we are an ageing population, and old age is a risk factor for dementia, a major concern for baby boomers is the issue of brain ageing and how to prevent it. A review of international research has identified some positive dietary changes that can be adopted to decrease the risk of developing Alzheimer's disease and help keep our brains healthy.

Keeping saturated-fat intake low is important because cholesterol-clogged blood vessels in the brain can increase the risk of stroke and result in vascular dementia. Boosting our intake of antioxidant foods appears to be highly protective. This is because damage to nerve cells in the brain may be caused, in part, by the production of free radicals.

A high-antioxidant diet is recommended throughout life. Choose a variety and include a colourful array of vegetables and fruits – of particular interest is the anthocyanin-rich blueberry (see *hero foods*, page 22). Prunes, also, are one of the highest antioxidant foods.

The antioxidant vitamin, vitamin E, has been widely studied in relation to brain function and vitamin E-rich foods such as nuts and nut oils, and cruciferous vegetables, such as cauliflower and broccoli, and kiwifruit and avocado could also be protective.

It is not fully known whether two of the B vitamins, vitamin B12 and folate, reduce the risk of dementia, however, they are both necessary for cell function, and low levels of both have been associated with impaired cognition (the loss of the ability to think, reason and remember) and a higher incidence of dementia.

Folate is found in many fresh fruits and vegetables, fortified breakfast cereals and Vegemite, while vitamin B12 is found primarily in animal products, such as lean meat, fish, poultry, eggs and dairy products like milk, cheese and yogurt.

daily servings **and serving sizes**

The Australian Guide to Healthy Eating recommends you choose the number of daily servings you need from the food groups according to your level of physical activity and body size. If you don't do much exercise, or are of small to average size, you should use the lower number. If you are active, or of average to large size, you should use the higher number.

food group	daily servings	a good source of	1 serving equals
bread, cereals, rice, pasta, noodles	women 4-6 men 5-7	This food group is rich in the B vitamins folate, thiamin, riboflavin and niacin. It also provides fibre and carbohydrates – wholemeal varieties are richer in fibre than refined.	2 slices of bread or 1 medium bread roll 1 cup cooked rice, pasta or noodles 1 cup porridge, ½ cup muesli or 1⅓ cups breakfast cereal flakes
vegetables and legumes	women 4-7 men 6-8	Foods in this group are good sources of vitamins, minerals, dietary fibre and carbohydrates.	½ cup cooked vegetables ½ cup cooked beans, lentils, chickpeas, split peas or canned beans 1 cup salad vegetables 1 cooked spotato
fruit	women 2-3 men 3-4	Foods in this group are a good source of vitamins especially vitamin C and the B vitamin, folate.	1 medium-sized apple, banana, orange or pear 2 small apricots, kiwifruit or plums 1 cup diced or canned fruit
milk, yogurt, cheese	women 2-3 men 2-4	This food group is an excellent source of calcium.	1 cup fresh milk (250ml) ½ cup evaporated milk (125ml) 2 slices cheese (40g) 1 small carton yogurt (200g) 1 cup custard (250ml)
meat, fish, poultry, eggs, nuts	women 1-1½ men 1½-2	This food group is a good source of protein, niacin and vitamin B12 and a particularly good source of the minerals iron and zinc.	65-100g cooked meat or chicken e.g., ½ cup lean mince, 2 small chops or 2 slices roast meat 80-100g cooked fish fillets ⅓ cup peanuts or almonds ¼ cup sunflower seeds or sesame seeds
fats and oils	women 0-2½ men 0-3	Unsaturated fats may help lower cholesterol levels, while saturated fats can increase the risk of heart disease. (See *the facts on fat*, page 10, for more detail.)	1 tablespoon (20g) butter, margarine, oil

wellbeing weight loss meal plan

This meal plan has been designed as a guide for anyone wanting to lose weight the wellbeing way. It's been structured to provide a balance of the food groups and average vitamin and mineral requirements, while the total fat and kilojoule count has been reduced. By following the 7-day plan in conjunction with regular physical activity, you could expect to lose weight safely at a rate of ½-1kg per week.

	Breakfast	Snack	Lunch	Snack	Dinner	Snack
MONDAY	Almond, date and cinnamon couscous, p34	1 apple	Focaccia with roasted capsicum, grilled eggplant and low-fat fetta cheese	1 cup blueberries	Pepita sesame cutlets with mint and parsley salad, p80, *plus* 1 cup steamed rice	200g low-fat fruit yogurt
TUESDAY	1⅓ cups iron-fortified wholegrain breakfast cereal with low-fat milk plus ½ grapefruit	4 rye crispbread with cottage cheese, cucumber and caper dip, p39	Spicy sardines with orange and olive salad, p66	200ml low-fat drinking yogurt	Moussaka stacks, p90, *plus* a garden salad	2 kiwifruit or other small fruit
WEDNESDAY	Pear smoothie, p43	Fruit-filled grain bar	Wholegrain roll with 2 slices turkey breast, avocado, cucumber and tomato chutney	¼ cup dried fruit and coconut trail mix, p40	Mixed pea and leek risotto p54, *plus* a garden salad	Pineapple and kiwifruit salad in basil lemon syrup, p108
THURSDAY	2 slices wholegrain toast with 2 teaspoons nut spread plus ½ grapefruit	200g low-fat yogurt	Black bean, corn and papaya salad, p54, *plus* 4 rye crispbread topped with 2 slices low-fat cheese	2 cups strawberries	Salmon en papillote, p75	Lime sorbet, p105
FRIDAY	Oatcakes with honeyed ricotta and blueberries, p30, *plus* 1 cup low-fat milk	2 apricots or other small fruit	1 large mountain bread wrap with 2 slices lean roast beef, 1 tablespoon hummus, tomato and spinach leaves, *plus* 1 orange	3 cups air-popped popcorn	Chicken, mixed vegies and almond stir-fry, p80	200g low-fat fruit yogurt
SATURDAY	Breakfast burrito, p28	Café latté or hot chocolate made with low-fat milk	Ocean trout tartare, p75	1 pear *plus* 2 slices low-fat cheese	Mushroom, beef and barley casserole, p94	3 fresh figs *plus* 4 squares dark chocolate
SUNDAY	Smoked salmon and poached egg on rye, p30	1 banana blended with 1 cup low-fat milk	Grilled moroccan lamb with burghul salad, p62	1 orange	Vegetable and lentil lasagne, p52	Pear, rhubarb and ricotta tart, p106

breakfasts

breakfast burrito

preparation time 25 minutes
cooking time 20 minutes serves 4
per serving 1810kJ (433 cal); 26.6g total fat (9.7g saturated fat); 27.7g carbohydrate; 16.3g protein; 9.1g fibre

250g cherry tomatoes
2 teaspoons olive oil
420g can kidney beans, rinsed, drained
⅓ cup coarsely chopped fresh flat-leaf parsley
1 tablespoon coarsely chopped pickled jalapeño chilli
1 tablespoon lime juice
1 large avocado (320g)
8 corn tortillas, warmed
50g baby spinach leaves
1 cup (120g) coarsely grated cheddar cheese

1 Preheat grill.
2 Combine tomatoes and oil in small shallow flameproof dish; grill about 15 minutes or until tomatoes have softened.
3 Combine beans, parsley, chilli and half the lime juice in medium bowl with tomatoes.
4 Mash avocado in small bowl with remaining lime juice.
5 Serve warmed tortillas topped with bean mixture, avocado, spinach leaves and cheese.

did you know? People who eat breakfast have more nutritious diets than people who skip it. Breakfast-eaters have lower intakes of fat, higher fibre intakes and are more likely to meet the recommended dietary intakes (RDI), i.e., the amount of specific nutrients required in one day for good health.

oatcakes with honeyed ricotta and blueberries

preparation time 15 minutes
cooking time 15 minutes **serves** 4
per serving 1547kJ (370 cal); 11.1g total fat (6.4g saturated fat); 51.8g carbohydrate; 13.9g protein; 5.5g fibre

Oatmeal, also sold as oatmeal flour, is made from milled oat kernels; it is not the same product as rolled oats or oat bran. It is available at health food stores.

⅔ cup (100g) wholemeal self-raising flour
1½ teaspoons baking powder
½ teaspoon ground cinnamon
½ cup (70g) oatmeal
2 egg whites
¾ cup (180ml) buttermilk
2 tablespoons honey
20g butter, melted
⅓ cup (60g) fresh blueberries

honeyed ricotta
⅔ cup (130g) ricotta cheese
1 teaspoon finely grated lemon rind
2 tablespoons honey

1 Make honeyed ricotta.
2 Sift flour, baking powder and cinnamon into medium bowl; stir in oatmeal. Gradually whisk in combined egg whites, buttermilk and honey; stir in butter.
3 Pour ¼ cup batter into heated lightly greased small frying pan; cook oatcake about 2 minutes or until bubbles appear. Turn oatcake; cook until lightly browned on other side. Repeat with remaining batter.
4 Serve oatcakes with honeyed ricotta and blueberries.

honeyed ricotta Combine ingredients in small bowl.

smoked salmon and poached egg on rye

preparation time 5 minutes
cooking time 4 minutes **serves** 4
per serving 1175kJ (281 cal); 8.8g total fat (2.2g saturated fat); 24.5g carbohydrate; 23.7g protein; 4.1g fibre

4 eggs
170g asparagus, halved crossways
4 slices (180g) rye bread, toasted
200g smoked salmon
2 tablespoons fresh chervil leaves

1 Half fill large shallow frying pan with water; bring to a boil. Break eggs into cup, one at a time, then slide into pan. When all eggs are in pan, allow water to return to a boil.
2 Cover pan, turn off heat; stand about 4 minutes or until a light film sets over egg yolks. Remove eggs, one at a time, using slotted spoon; place spoon on absorbent-paper-lined saucer briefly to blot up poaching liquid.
3 Meanwhile, boil, steam or microwave asparagus until just tender; drain.
4 Divide bread among serving plates; top each with salmon, egg then asparagus; sprinkle with chervil.

oatcakes with honeyed ricotta and blueberries

smoked salmon and poached egg on rye

did you know? Cholesterol is made by your body, and is vital for normal cell fuction, as well as hormone and vitamin D production. Your cholesterol level is also influenced by the food you eat; your body can make too much cholesterol if you eat too much saturated fat (found in animal-based foods such as meat and dairy products).

wholemeal banana and prune bread

bircher muesli with figs and pistachios

did you know? Children who eat an inadequate breakfast are more likely to make poor food choices the rest of the day, and in the long-term as well. Eating breakfast also can have a significant effect on learning, with students more interested and better able to pay attention and retain information.

wholemeal banana and prune bread

preparation time 15 minutes
cooking time 1 hour **serves** 12
per serving 1066kJ (255 cal); 8.2g total fat (4.8g saturated fat); 39.6g carbohydrate; 4.6g protein; 4.2g fibre

You need three large overripe bananas (600g) for this recipe.

- 1½ cups (240g) wholemeal self-raising flour
- 1 teaspoon ground cinnamon
- 2 teaspoons finely grated lemon rind
- 100g butter, softened
- ¾ cup (165g) firmly packed dark brown sugar
- 2 eggs
- 1½ cups mashed banana
- 1 cup (170g) seeded prunes, chopped coarsely

1 Preheat oven to 180°C/160°C fan-forced. Grease 14cm x 21cm loaf pan; line base and long sides with baking paper.
2 Sift flour and cinnamon into large bowl; add rind, butter, sugar and eggs. Beat with electric mixer on low speed until ingredients are combined. Increase speed to medium; beat mixture until smooth. Stir in banana and prunes.
3 Spread mixture into pan; bake about 1 hour. Stand bread in pan 5 minutes; turn onto wire rack to cool.

bircher muesli with figs and pistachios

preparation time 10 minutes (plus refrigeration time)
cooking time 5 minutes **serves** 4
per serving 1818kJ (435 cal); 14.5g total fat (2.9g saturated fat); 56.1g carbohydrate; 15.1g protein; 10.4g fibre

- 1½ cups (135g) rolled oats
- ¼ cup (30g) oat bran
- ¼ cup (15g) natural bran flakes
- ¾ cup (180ml) milk
- ¾ cup (180ml) orange juice
- ¾ cup (200g) low-fat greek-style yogurt
- ½ cup (100g) finely chopped dried figs
- ½ teaspoon ground cinnamon
- ½ cup (70g) roasted pistachios, chopped coarsely
- 1 large orange (300g), segmented

1 Combine cereals, milk, juice, yogurt, figs and cinnamon in large bowl. Cover; refrigerate overnight. Stir in half the nuts.
2 Divide muesli among serving bowls; top with orange segments and remaining nuts.

almond, date and cinnamon couscous

preparation time 10 minutes (plus cooling time)
cooking time 5 minutes **serves** 4
per serving 1313kJ (314 cal); 3.5g total fat (0.3g saturated fat); 57.9g carbohydrate; 9.9g protein; 4.8g fibre

1 cup (250ml) apple juice
½ cup (100g) couscous
2 tablespoons roasted slivered almonds
¾ cup (105g) coarsely chopped dried dates
1 cup (280g) low-fat vanilla yogurt
¼ teaspoon ground cinnamon
2 medium oranges (480g), segmented

1 Place juice in small saucepan; bring to a boil. Remove from heat.
2 Add couscous, cover; stand about 5 minutes or until juice is absorbed, fluffing with fork occasionally.
3 Stir nuts and dates into couscous. Serve couscous topped with yogurt. Sprinkle with cinnamon then top with orange segments.

baked eggs with herbs and fetta

preparation time 10 minutes
cooking time 10 minutes **serves** 4
per serving 1083kJ (259 cal); 19.7g total fat (9.2g saturated fat); 0.6g carbohydrate; 20.4g protein; 0.2g fibre

1 tablespoon finely chopped fresh flat-leaf parsley
1 tablespoon finely chopped fresh mint
1 green onion, sliced thinly
8 eggs
100g firm fetta cheese, crumbled
⅓ cup (40g) coarsely grated cheddar cheese

1 Preheat oven to 180°C/160°C fan-forced. Grease four ¾-cup (180ml) shallow ovenproof dishes.
2 Divide herbs and onion among dishes; break two eggs into each dish, sprinkle with combined cheeses. Bake, uncovered, about 10 minutes or until eggs are just set.

almond, date and cinnamon couscous

baked eggs with herbs and fetta

did you know? Research shows skipping breakfast is associated with a significantly higher risk of obesity. People who regularly skip breakfast had 4.5 times the risk of obesity as those who normally ate breakfast.

snacks

avocado, olive and bocconcini bruschetta

preparation time 15 minutes
cooking time 5 minutes **serves** 4
per serving 1693kJ (405 cal); 28.8g total fat (6.8g saturated fat); 24.4g carbohydrate; 10.1g protein; 4.5g fibre

¼ cup (60ml) olive oil
2 cloves garlic, crushed
4 slices (180g) wholegrain bread
1 medium avocado (250g), chopped coarsely
100g bocconcini cheese, chopped coarsely
¼ cup (30g) seeded black olives, chopped coarsely
1 tablespoon lemon juice
2 medium tomatoes (300g), chopped coarsely

1 Preheat grill.
2 Combine half the oil and half the garlic in small bowl. Brush both sides of bread with garlic oil; toast under hot grill until browned lightly both sides.
3 Combine avocado, cheese, olives, juice, tomato and remaining oil and garlic in medium bowl.
4 Serve bruschetta topped with avocado mixture.

did you know? US research has shown that successful long-term weight-loss participants are smart snackers, commonly eating 5-6 times per day.

clockwise from top: watercress and yogurt dip; cottage cheese, cucumber and caper dip; white bean and garlic dip

white bean and garlic dip

preparation time 5 minutes **makes** 1 cup
per ¼ cup 138kJ (33 cal); 0.9g total fat (0.6g saturated fat); 2.6g carbohydrate; 2.4g protein; 1.1g fibre

300g can white beans, rinsed, drained
⅓ cup (95g) yogurt
2 tablespoons lemon juice
1 clove garlic, quartered
¼ teaspoon ground cumin

1 Blend or process beans, yogurt, juice and garlic until smooth. Sprinkle dip with cumin.
2 Serve with raw vegetable sticks.

watercress and yogurt dip

preparation time 10 minutes **makes** 1 cup
per ¼ cup 222kJ (53 cal); 2.4g total fat (1.5g saturated fat); 3.4g carbohydrate; 3.6g protein; 0.4g fibre

1 cup loosely packed fresh watercress leaves
1 teaspoon ground cumin
¼ teaspoon cayenne pepper
1 cup (280g) yogurt

1 Blend or process watercress, spices and 2 tablespoons of the yogurt until smooth; transfer mixture to small bowl, stir in remaining yogurt.
2 Serve with raw vegetable sticks.

cottage cheese, cucumber and caper dip

preparation time 10 minutes **makes** 1 cup
per ¼ cup 238kJ (57 cal); 2.2g total fat (1.4g saturated fat); 3g carbohydrate; 6g protein; 0.5g fibre

¾ cup (150g) cottage cheese
½ lebanese cucumber (65g), seeded, chopped finely
½ small red onion (50g), chopped finely
1 tablespoon finely chopped dill cucumbers
1 tablespoon drained baby capers, rinsed
1 tablespoon finely chopped fresh mint leaves

1 Combine ingredients in small bowl.
2 Serve with raw vegetable sticks.

did you know? It's vital to build up the body's calcium bank early in life. Approximately 60 per cent of the weight of mature bone is made up of minerals, like calcium, that are continuously laid down during growth. Snacking on dairy foods is a great way to help get your 3-4 servings a day.

craisin, oatmeal and cinnamon scones

preparation time 10 minutes
cooking time 25 minutes **makes** 12
per scone 836kJ (200 cal); 6.1g total fat (3.5g saturated fat); 27.6g carbohydrate; 7g protein; 3.5g fibre

- 1 cup (160g) wholemeal self-raising flour
- 1 cup (150g) self-raising flour
- ½ cup (70g) fine oatmeal
- 1 teaspoon ground cinnamon
- ½ teaspoon finely grated lemon rind
- 30g butter
- ¾ cup (105g) craisins
- 1 cup (250ml) milk
- 2 tablespoons honey
- 1 tablespoon milk, extra
- 1 tablespoon oatmeal, extra
- 1 cup (200g) ricotta cheese

1 Preheat oven to 220°C/200°C fan-forced. Grease and flour deep 19cm-square cake pan.
2 Combine flours, oatmeal, cinnamon and rind in large bowl; rub in butter.
3 Stir in craisins, milk and honey.
4 Knead dough on floured surface until smooth. Press dough to a 2cm-thickness. Cut twelve 5.5cm rounds from dough; place in pan. Brush with extra milk then sprinkle with extra oatmeal. Bake about 25 minutes.
5 Serve scones warm with cheese, and honey, if desired.

dried fruit and coconut trail mix

preparation time 15 minutes
cooking time 10 minutes (plus cooling time) **makes** 3 cups
per ⅓ cup 869kJ (208 cal); 11.8g total fat (2.5g saturated fat); 20.7g carbohydrate; 4.2g protein; 3.7g fibre

- 2 tablespoons honey
- 2 teaspoons olive oil
- ¼ teaspoon mixed spice
- ½ cup (70g) pistachios
- ½ cup (80g) almond kernels
- ½ cup (25g) toasted flaked coconut
- ½ cup (65g) craisins
- ½ cup (75g) coarsely chopped dried apricots
- ½ cup (70g) coarsely chopped dried dates

1 Preheat oven to 180°C/160°C fan-forced.
2 Combine honey, oil and spice in small bowl.
3 Combine nuts in shallow baking dish; drizzle with honey mixture. Roast, uncovered, about 10 minutes or until browned lightly, stirring halfway through cooking time. Cool 15 minutes.
4 Stir in remaining ingredients; cool.

craisin, oatmeal and cinnamon scones

dried fruit and coconut trail mix

did you know? Children need to eat mini meals throughout the day. Most children can snack up to 5 or 6 times a day, thanks to their small stomach capacity and large appetites, providing them with a third to a half of their energy needs.

drinks

did you know? Absorption of iron can be increased up to four times by pairing with a vitamin C-rich food in the same meal. Good matches include an iron-fortified cereal and orange juice at breakfast or, for a main meal, try tomato salad with steak, or red capsicum in a lamb stir-fry.

pomegranate and orange

preparation time 10 minutes
makes 1 cup (250ml)
per 250ml 1112kJ (266 cal); 0.7g total fat (0g saturated fat); 49.2g carbohydrate; 6.8g protein; 17.1g fibre

You need two large pomegranates to get the amount of pulp required here.

⅔ cup (160ml) pomegranate pulp
2 medium oranges (480g), peeled, quartered

1 Push ingredients through juice extractor into glass; stir to combine.

pineapple and orange

preparation time 5 minutes
makes 1 litre (4 cups)
per 250ml 815kJ (195 cal); 0.4g total fat (0g saturated fat); 38.5g carbohydrate; 4.5g protein; 8.5g fibre

1 medium pineapple (1kg), peeled, chopped coarsely
6 medium oranges (1.5kg), peeled, quartered
5cm piece fresh horseradish (25g)
1 tablespoon honey

1 Push fruit and horseradish through juice extractor into glass.
2 Add honey; stir to combine.

red grape spritzer

preparation time 5 minutes
makes 1 litre (4 cups)
per 250ml 715kJ (171 cal); 0.3g total fat (0g saturated fat); 37.4g carbohydrate; 3.1g protein; 2.3g fibre

1kg seedless red grapes
2½ cups (625ml) soda water
1 tablespoon lime juice
8 fresh mint leaves, shredded

1 Push grapes through juice extractor into glass; stir in soda water, juice and mint.

pear smoothie

preparation time 5 minutes
makes 1 litre (4 cups)
per 250ml 589kJ (141 cal); 2.8g total fat (0g saturated fat); 25.5g carbohydrate; 1.9g protein; 2.6g fibre

2 medium pears (460g)
2 cups (500ml) soy milk
1 tablespoon honey

1 Peel and core pears then chop coarsely.
2 Blend or process ingredients until smooth.

zesty beetroot

preparation time 5 minutes
makes 1 litre (4 cups)
per 250ml 617kJ (147 cal); 0.5g total fat (0g saturated fat); 24.5g carbohydrate; 5.8g protein; 10.4g fibre

You need 2kg of silver beet to get the required amount of trimmed leaves.

3 medium beetroots (525g), chopped coarsely
4 medium oranges (960g), peeled, quartered
500g trimmed silver beet
1 cup (250ml) water
1 fresh small red thai chilli, chopped finely

1 Push beetroot, orange and silver beet through juice extractor into glass. Stir in the water.
2 Add chilli; stand 5 minutes. Strain mixture through fine sieve into large jug.

cranberry cooler

preparation time 5 minutes
makes 1 litre (4 cups)
per 250ml 134kJ (32 cal); 0.2g total fat (0g saturated fat); 6.6g carbohydrate; 0.3g protein; 1.2g fibre

1⅓ cups (150g) frozen cranberries, thawed
1kg watermelon, peeled, chopped coarsely
2 lebanese cucumbers (260g), chopped coarsely
2 medium pears (460g), chopped coarsely

1 Push ingredients through juice extractor into glass; stir to combine.

ruby red citrus

preparation time 5 minutes
makes 1 litre (4 cups)
per 250ml 579kJ (138 cal); 0.4g total fat (0g saturated fat); 28.3g carbohydrate; 2.8g protein; 4.4g fibre

2 medium ruby red grapefruits (700g), peeled, quartered
3 large oranges (900g), peeled, quartered
1 medium lemon (140g), peeled, quartered
1 cup (250ml) water
2 tablespoons honey

1 Push fruit through juice extractor into glass. Add the water and honey; stir to combine.

chlorophyll booster

preparation time 5 minutes
makes 1 litre (4 cups)
per 250ml 815kJ (195 cal); 0.9g total fat (0g saturated fat); 37.8g carbohydrate; 5g protein; 7g fibre

Most domestic juicers do not include a wheatgrass extractor; this needs to be bought separately. However, if you have a wheatgrass juicer, you need about 40g of fresh wheatgrass for this recipe. Alternatively, purchase a 30ml shot of wheatgrass from your local juice bar or health food shop.

1 medium cos lettuce, trimmed
1kg seedless green grapes
30ml wheatgrass shot
1 cup (250ml) water

1 Push lettuce and grapes through juice extractor into glass. Add wheatgrass shot and the water; stir to combine.

cashew milk with rosewater and cardamom

preparation time 5 minutes (plus standing and refrigeration time)
makes 1 litre (4 cups)
per 250ml 3082kJ (736 cal); 57.7g total fat (9.8g saturated fat); 34.6g carbohydrate; 18.8g protein; 4.8g fibre

1.5 litres (6 cups) water
3 cups (450g) unsalted cashews
1 tablespoon honey
3 cardamom pods, bruised
1 teaspoon rosewater
1 teaspoon vanilla extract

1 Blend or process the water, nuts and honey, in batches, until smooth. Add cardamom pods; stand 2 hours.
2 Strain mixture through muslin-lined sieve into large jug; discard solids. Stir in rosewater and extract; refrigerate before serving.

honeydew, papaya and orange

preparation time 5 minutes
makes 1 litre (4 cups)
per 250ml 150kJ (36 cal); 0.2g total fat (0g saturated fat); 6.9g carbohydrate; 0.7g protein; 1.5g fibre

1 medium honeydew melon (1.5 kg), peeled, chopped coarsely
1 small papaya (650g), peeled, chopped coarsely
3 medium oranges (720g), peeled, quartered

1 Push fruit through juice extractor into glass; stir to combine.

vegetables

tofu zucchini patties

preparation time 15 minutes
cooking time 15 minutes **serves** 4
per serving 1831kJ (438 cal); 18.8g total fat (3.2g saturated fat); 43.2g carbohydrate; 19.8g protein; 6.6g fibre

You need to cook ⅔ cup (130g) of brown rice for this recipe.

- 300g firm silken tofu, chopped coarsely
- 1½ cups cooked brown rice
- 3 medium zucchini (360g), grated coarsely
- 1 medium brown onion (150g), chopped finely
- 1 cup (100g) packaged breadcrumbs
- 2 eggs
- 2 tablespoons finely chopped fresh flat-leaf parsley
- 1 clove garlic, crushed
- 2 tablespoons olive oil
- 2 lemons, cut into wedges

1 Blend or process tofu until smooth; transfer to large bowl. Add rice, zucchini, onion, breadcrumbs, eggs, parsley and garlic; mix well. Shape mixture into 12 patties.

2 Heat oil in large frying pan; cook patties, in batches, about 3 minutes each side or until browned and heated through. Drain on absorbent paper. Serve patties with lemon wedges and, if desired, watercress and yogurt.

did you know? Soy foods like tofu contain types of phytoestrogens known as isoflavones. These are naturally-occurring plant chemicals that mimic the action of the oestrogen hormone, and they have been reported to be beneficial for some women. It's important to note, however, that dietary phytoestrogens are much weaker than oestrogen produced naturally in the body.

chive wontons with choy sum in asian broth

preparation time 40 minutes
(plus standing time)
cooking time 15 minutes **serves** 6
per serving 782kJ (187 cal); 3.2g total fat
(0.7g saturated fat); 27g carbohydrate;
10.9g protein; 2.2g fibre

150g firm silken tofu
500g choy sum, trimmed
2 tablespoons finely chopped fresh chives
190g can water chestnuts, rinsed, drained, chopped finely
2 fresh long red chillies, chopped finely
30 wonton wrappers
1 litre (4 cups) vegetable stock
1 litre (4 cups) water
10cm stick fresh lemon grass (20g), chopped coarsely
2cm piece fresh ginger (10g), chopped coarsely
1 clove garlic, quartered
2 kaffir lime leaves
¼ cup (60ml) light soy sauce

1 Dry tofu with absorbent paper then chop coarsely. Stand tofu on several layers of absorbent paper, cover with more paper; stand for 20 minutes. Chop finely.
2 Chop a quarter of the choy sum finely. Combine in medium bowl with tofu, chives, water chestnut and half the chilli.
3 Centre level tablespoons of tofu mixture on a wrapper. Brush wrapper edges with water; gather edges above filling, pinching together to seal. Repeat process with remaining wrappers and filling.
4 Combine stock, the water, lemon grass, ginger, garlic, lime leaves, sauce and remaining chilli in large saucepan; bring to a boil. Reduce heat; simmer, uncovered, 5 minutes. Strain into large bowl; discard solids.
5 Return broth to pan; bring to a boil; cook wontons, in two batches, about 4 minutes or until cooked through. Transfer wontons to individual serving bowls.
6 Cook remaining choy sum in broth until just tender. Divide choy sum among bowls then ladle broth over choy sum and wontons.

grilled zucchini with pumpkin and couscous

preparation time 20 minutes
cooking time 20 minutes **serves** 4
per serving 1200kJ (287 cal); 12.7g total fat (2.5g saturated fat); 30.1g carbohydrate; 10.1g protein; 4.9g fibre

½ cup (100g) couscous
½ cup (125ml) boiling water
2 tablespoons lemon juice
2 teaspoons olive oil
¼ cup (40g) pine nuts
1 clove garlic, crushed
½ small red onion (50g), chopped finely
1 teaspoon sweet smoked paprika
½ teaspoon ground cumin
½ teaspoon cayenne pepper
½ small red capsicum (75g), chopped finely
200g piece pumpkin, chopped finely
2 tablespoons finely chopped fresh flat-leaf parsley
6 medium zucchini (720g), halved lengthways

preserved lemon yogurt
½ cup (140g) greek-style yogurt
2 tablespoons finely chopped preserved lemon
2 tablespoons water

1 Make preserved lemon yogurt.
2 Combine couscous with the water and juice in large heatproof bowl, cover; stand about 5 minutes or until water is absorbed, fluffing with fork occasionally.
3 Heat oil in large saucepan; cook nuts, stirring, until browned lightly. Add garlic, onion and spices; cook, stirring, until onion softens. Add capsicum and pumpkin; cook, stirring, until pumpkin is just tender. Stir in couscous and parsley.
4 Meanwhile, cook zucchini on heated oiled grill plate (or grill or barbecue) until just tender.
5 Serve zucchini topped with couscous and drizzled with yogurt.

preserved lemon yogurt Combine ingredients in small bowl.

vegetable and lentil lasagne

preparation time 15 minutes
cooking time 45 minutes **serves** 4
per serving 1898kJ (454 cal); 22.1g total fat (8.9g saturated fat); 34.3g carbohydrate; 26g protein; 10.8g fibre

Use scissors to trim lasagne sheets to fit into the baking dishes.

1 cup (200g) red lentils
2 tablespoons olive oil
1 small leek (200g), sliced thinly
1 fresh long red chilli, chopped finely
2 cloves garlic, crushed
4 medium tomatoes (600g), chopped coarsely
1 tablespoon tomato paste
4 fresh lasagne sheets
50g baby spinach leaves
200g ricotta cheese
100g firm fetta cheese, crumbled
1 tablespoon finely chopped fresh basil

1 Preheat oven to 200°C/180°C fan-forced. Oil four 1½-cup (375ml) ovenproof dishes.

2 Cook lentils in large saucepan of boiling water, uncovered, until just tender; drain.

3 Meanwhile, heat half the oil in large saucepan; cook leek, chilli and garlic, stirring, until leek softens. Add tomato and paste; cook, stirring, until liquid is almost absorbed. Remove from heat; stir in lentils.

4 Spoon 1 tablespoon of lentil mixture into each dish; cover each with trimmed lasagne. Divide half the remaining lentil mixture among dishes; top each with equal amounts of spinach then ricotta. Cover ricotta with trimmed lasagne; top each with remaining lentil mixture then sprinkle with fetta.

5 Bake lasagne, uncovered, about 20 minutes or until heated through. Stand 5 minutes; sprinkle each lasagne with basil and remaining oil.

did you know? Carrots can help you see in the dark as they are one of the richest sources of vitamin A. This "vision vitamin" helps prevent night blindness. Vitamin A deficiency is the most common cause of blindness in young children.

mixed pea and leek risotto

preparation time 20 minutes
cooking time 40 minutes **serves** 4
per serving 2211kJ (529 cal); 8.7g total fat (2.5g saturated fat); 90.2g carbohydrate; 18.1g protein; 7.1g fibre

1 litre (4 cups) vegetable stock
2 cups (500ml) water
1 tablespoon olive oil
1 medium leek (350g), sliced thinly
2 cups (400g) arborio rice
1 cup (120g) frozen peas
250g snow peas, trimmed, halved lengthways
250g sugar snap peas, trimmed
2 tablespoons coarsely chopped fresh mint
2 tablespoons coarsely chopped fresh flat-leaf parsley
2 tablespoons finely chopped fresh chives
1 tablespoon finely grated lemon rind
⅓ cup (25g) grated parmesan

1 Combine stock and the water in large saucepan; bring to a boil, simmer, covered.
2 Heat oil in large saucepan; cook leek, stirring, until softened. Stir in rice. Add ½ cup simmering stock mixture; cook, stirring, over low heat, until liquid is absorbed. Continue adding stock mixture, in ½-cup batches, stirring until liquid is absorbed after each addition. Total cooking time should be about 30 minutes.
3 Add frozen peas to risotto; cook, stirring, until tender. Stir in remaining peas; remove from heat, stir in herbs, rind and cheese.

black bean, corn and papaya salad

preparation time 30 minutes (plus standing time)
cooking time 45 minutes **serves** 4
per serving 711kJ (170 cal); 9.9g total fat (1.4g saturated fat); 13g carbohydrate; 4.4g protein; 5.4g fibre

You need to buy half a small papaya weighing about 325g for this recipe. We used the red-fleshed Fijian papaya.

1 cup (200g) dried black beans
1 trimmed corn cob (250g)
5 medium egg tomatoes (375g), seeded
4 green onions, sliced thinly
1 cup (170g) diced papaya
⅓ cup coarsely chopped fresh coriander
4 large iceberg lettuce leaves

lime dressing
1 clove garlic, crushed
2 tablespoons lime juice
2 tablespoons olive oil
1 tablespoon white wine vinegar
½ teaspoon white sugar
1 fresh small red thai chilli, chopped finely

1 Cover beans with cold water in medium bowl; stand overnight, drain. Rinse beans under cold water; drain. Cook beans in medium saucepan of boiling water, uncovered, until beans are just tender. Drain.
2 Meanwhile, microwave, steam or grill corn until tender; cut kernels from cobs.
3 Blend or process tomato until just finely chopped.
4 Make lime dressing.
5 Combine beans, corn and tomato in large bowl with onion, papaya, coriander and dressing. Divide salad among lettuce leaves.

lime dressing Combine ingredients in screw-top jar; shake well.

mixed pea and leek risotto

black bean, corn and papaya salad

creamy barley and mixed mushroom pilaf

preparation time 25 minutes
cooking time 55 minutes **serves** 4
per serving 1195kJ (286 cal); 11.2g total fat (6g saturated fat); 28.1g carbohydrate; 10.4g protein; 9.5g fibre

2 cups (500ml) vegetable stock
3 cups (750ml) water
40g butter
150g button mushrooms, sliced thinly
150g swiss brown mushrooms, sliced thinly
150g oyster mushrooms, sliced thinly
1 teaspoon olive oil
1 medium brown onion (150g), chopped finely
2 cloves garlic, crushed
¾ cup (150g) pearl barley
⅓ cup (80ml) dry white wine
100g enoki mushrooms
½ cup coarsely chopped fresh garlic chives
¼ cup coarsely chopped fresh flat-leaf parsley

1 Combine stock and the water in medium saucepan; bring to a boil, simmer, covered.

2 Heat butter in large deep frying pan; cook button, swiss and oyster mushrooms, stirring, 5 minutes or until tender. Remove from pan.

3 Heat oil in same pan; cook onion and garlic, stirring, until onion softens. Stir in barley. Add wine; cook, stirring, until liquid has almost evaporated. Add ½ cup simmering stock mixture; cook, stirring, over low heat until liquid is absorbed. Continue adding stock mixture, in ½-cup batches, stirring until absorbed after each addition. Total cooking time should be about 40 minutes or until barley is just tender.

4 Remove from heat; stir in mushroom mixture, enoki mushrooms and herbs.

did you know? Kumara are a good source of low-GI carbohydrate, as well as being packed with antioxidant vitamins. They supply more beta-carotene, the precursor to vitamin A, than any other vegetable. Kumara are also an excellent source of vitamins C and E, helping to beat free-radical damage and fight disease.

salads

chipotle, corn, tomato and chickpea salad

preparation time 20 minutes (plus standing time)
cooking time 15 minutes **serves** 4
per serving 853kJ (204 cal); 2.9g total fat (0.3g saturated fat); 30.5g carbohydrate; 9.5g protein; 9.4g fibre

Chipotle, pronounced "cheh-pote-lay", is the name given to jalapeño chillies once they've been dried and smoked. Having a deep, intensely smoky flavour rather than a searing heat, chipotles must be rehydrated before use.

1 chipotle chilli
2 tablespoons boiling water
½ cup (130g) bottled tomato pasta sauce
1 tablespoon lime juice
1 teaspoon ground cumin
2 trimmed corn cobs (500g)
420g can chickpeas, drained, rinsed
250g cherry tomatoes, halved
1 small red onion (100g), sliced thinly
1 cup loosely packed fresh coriander leaves

1 Place chilli and the water in small bowl; stand 15 minutes. Discard stalk; blend or process chilli, soaking liquid and sauce until mixture is smooth. Transfer to small bowl; stir in lime juice.
2 Dry-fry cumin in small frying pan, stirring, until fragrant; stir into chilli sauce mixture.
3 Cook corn on heated oiled grill plate (or grill or barbecue) until browned lightly and tender. Cut kernels from cobs.
4 Combine chilli mixture and corn in large bowl with remaining ingredients.

did you know? A good way to ensure you keep hydrated during exercise is to monitor your sweat losses. Weigh yourself before and after activity to assess your body fluid losses. As a general rule, 1kg of weight loss quates to roughly 1 litre of lost fluid. Drink water before and during activity, and refresh afterwards with a juice or drinking yogurt. People doing strenuous activity will benefit from a sports drink.

asian millet and tofu salad

preparation time 20 minutes
cooking time 15 minutes **serves** 4
per serving 1676kJ (401 cal); 14.4g total fat (2.2g saturated fat); 39.3g carbohydrate; 22g protein; 8.8g fibre

We used cryovac-packed ready-to-serve sweet chilli tofu, available from many supermarkets and Asian food stores.

1 cup (200g) millet
2 fresh long red chillies, chopped finely
⅓ cup (45g) roasted unsalted coarsely chopped peanuts
400g firm marinated tofu, cut into batons
100g snow peas, trimmed, sliced lengthways
230g can bamboo shoots, rinsed, drained, sliced thinly
½ small red onion (50g), sliced thinly

mirin dressing
¼ cup (60ml) mirin
1 tablespoon japanese soy sauce
1 tablespoon rice vinegar
1 clove garlic, crushed

1 Cook millet in medium saucepan of boiling water, uncovered, until just tender; drain. Cool.
2 Meanwhile, make mirin dressing.
3 Combine millet in large bowl with chilli, nuts and half the dressing.
4 Combine remaining ingredients and dressing in medium bowl.
5 Serve millet mixture topped with tofu salad.

mirin dressing Place ingredients in screw-top jar; shake well.

japanese prawn and soba salad

preparation time 35 minutes (plus standing time)
cooking time 15 minutes **serves** 4
per serving 1329kJ (318 cal); 6.1g total fat (1.1g saturated fat); 37.7g carbohydrate; 25.4g protein; 3.9g fibre

Wakame is a bright-green seaweed used in soups, salads and seasonings. Usually sold dried, wakame can be rehydrated by soaking it in water for about 10 minutes; discard any hard stems. Good for general use, yellow miso, often called "shinshu", is a deep-yellow, smooth miso which is both salty and tart. Wakame and yellow miso are found in most Asian food stores.

200g dried soba noodles
10g dried wakame
1 medium carrot (120g)
1 lebanese cucumber (130g)
16 uncooked medium king prawns (720g)
½ sheet toasted nori, shredded finely

miso dressing
1 tablespoon water
2 tablespoons rice vinegar
1 tablespoon yellow miso
1 fresh long red chilli, chopped finely
2cm piece fresh ginger (10g), grated finely
1 clove garlic, crushed
1 tablespoon peanut oil

1 Cook noodles in medium saucepan of boiling water, uncovered, until just tender; drain. Rinse noodles under cold water; drain.
2 Place wakame in small bowl, cover with cold water; stand about 10 minutes or until softened. Drain then squeeze out excess water. Chop coarsely, removing hard ribs or stems.
3 Meanwhile, make miso dressing.
4 Using vegetable peeler, slice carrot and cucumber lengthways into thin ribbons.
5 Shell and devein prawns, leaving tails intact. Cook prawns in medium saucepan of boiling water, uncovered, until changed in colour. Drain on absorbent paper; cool.
6 Combine noodles, wakame, carrot, cucumber and prawns in large bowl with dressing. Serve salad sprinkled with nori.

miso dressing Place ingredients in screw-top jar; shake well.

asian millet and tofu salad

japanese prawn and soba salad

grilled moroccan lamb with burghul salad

preparation time 20 minutes
cooking time 20 minutes **serves** 4
per serving 2776kJ (664 cal); 30.7g total fat (6.3g saturated fat); 38.5g carbohydrate; 53g protein; 10.8g fibre

With a name that loosely translates as "top of the shop", ras el hanout is an aromatic Moroccan blend of the best a spice merchant has to offer: allspice, cumin, paprika, fennel, caraway and saffron are all generally part of the mix. It is available from Middle Eastern and specialty spice stores.

¾ cup (120g) burghul
1 tablespoon olive oil
1 tablespoon ras el hanout
800g lamb backstraps
½ cup (70g) roasted unsalted pistachios, chopped coarsely
1 small red onion (100g), chopped finely
¾ cup loosely packed fresh parsley leaves
¾ cup loosely packed fresh mint leaves
⅓ cup (55g) dried currants
1 tablespoons finely grated lemon rind
1 clove garlic, crushed
¼ cup (60ml) lemon juice
2 tablespoons olive oil, extra

1 Place burghul in medium bowl, cover with water. Stand 10 minutes; drain. Squeeze out as much excess water as possible.
2 Combine oil, spice and lamb in medium bowl, turn to coat lamb in mixture. Cook lamb, in batches, on heated oiled grill plate (or grill or barbecue) until browned both sides and cooked as desired. Cover lamb; stand 10 minutes then slice thickly.
3 Combine burghul in medium bowl with remaining ingredients; toss gently.
4 Serve salad topped with sliced lamb and, if desired, yogurt.

hot and sour green papaya and pork salad

preparation time 20 minutes
cooking time 25 minutes **serves** 4
per serving 1643kJ (393 cal); 11.4g total fat (2.3g saturated fat); 31.7g carbohydrate; 37.9g protein; 6.6g fibre

½ cup (125ml) water
600g pork fillets
1 small green papaya (650g)
1 large carrot (180g)
2 teaspoons vegetable oil
1 cup firmly packed fresh coriander leaves
⅓ cup (45g) coarsely chopped roasted unsalted peanuts

chilli and tamarind dressing
4 cloves garlic, crushed
4 fresh small red thai chillies, chopped finely
⅔ cup (200g) tamarind concentrate
1 tablespoon finely grated lime rind
½ cup (125ml) lime juice
2 shallots (50g), sliced thinly
⅓ cup grated palm sugar

1 Make chilli and tamarind dressing.
2 Place the water in large frying pan with ½ cup of the dressing. Add pork; bring to a boil. Reduce heat; simmer, covered, 20 minutes or until pork is cooked through. Remove pork from pan; cover, stand pork 10 minutes then slice thinly.
3 Peel then halve papaya; remove seeds. Using vegetable peeler, slice papaya and carrot lengthways into thin strips.
4 Stir oil into remaining dressing. Combine pork, papaya, carrot, coriander and dressing in medium bowl. Serve salad topped with nuts.

chilli and tamarind dressing
Combine ingredients in small jug.

grilled moroccan lamb with burghul salad

hot and sour green papaya and pork salad

cashew patty salad with spiced yogurt

preparation time 25 minutes
cooking time 10 minutes **serves** 4
per serving 2324kJ (556 cal); 37.1g total fat (7g saturated fat); 32.5g carbohydrate; 17.6g protein; 11.1g fibre

⅓ cup (55g) burghul
⅔ cup (160ml) boiling water
1½ cups (225g) roasted unsalted cashews
⅓ cup (50g) wholemeal plain flour
1 medium brown onion (150g), quartered
2 cloves garlic, halved
1⅓ cups firmly packed fresh flat-leaf parsley leaves
2 tablespoons vegetable oil
200g baby spinach leaves
1 lebanese cucumber (130g), chopped coarsely
250g cherry tomatoes, halved

spiced yogurt
1 cup (280g) yogurt
1 tablespoon lime juice
1 teaspoon ground cumin
2 green onions, chopped finely

1 Place burghul in medium heatproof bowl, add the water; stand 10 minutes.
2 Meanwhile, make spiced yogurt.
3 Blend or process nuts, flour, onion, garlic and ⅓ cup of the parsley until smooth. Combine with burghul mixture in medium bowl. Shape mixture into 24 patties.
4 Heat oil in large frying pan; cook patties, in batches, until browned all over and heated through.
5 Combine remaining parsley in large bowl with remaining ingredients. Serve salad topped with patties; drizzle with yogurt.
spiced yogurt Combine ingredients in small bowl.

cauliflower and green olive salad

preparation time 15 minutes
cooking time 5 minutes **serves** 4
per serving 1087kJ (260 cal); 17.2g total fat (6.1g saturated fat); 12.3g carbohydrate; 11.3g protein; 5.5g fibre

In this recipe, we used only the leaves from the inner stalks of celery. Pale in colour, these are not bitter as are the tougher outer leaves. Preserved lemons, salted lemons preserved in a mixture of olive oil and lemon juice, are available from specialty food shops and delicatessens.

1 small cauliflower (1kg), trimmed, cut into florets
1 cup (120g) large green olives, seeded, halved
1 trimmed celery stalk (100g), sliced thinly
1 cup loosely packed celery leaves
½ cup loosely packed fresh flat-leaf parsley leaves
1 small red onion (100g), sliced thinly
2 tablespoons lemon juice
1 tablespoon finely chopped preserved lemon
2 tablespoons olive oil
1 clove garlic, crushed
125g fetta cheese, crumbled

1 Boil, steam or microwave cauliflower until tender; drain.
2 Combine cauliflower in medium bowl with olives, celery, celery leaves, parsley, onion, juice, preserved lemon, oil and garlic.
3 Serve salad sprinkled with cheese.

cashew patty salad with spiced yogurt

cauliflower and green olive salad

seafood

spicy sardines with orange and olive salad

preparation time 20 minutes
cooking time 15 minutes **serves** 4
per serving 2500kJ (598 cal); 36.2g total fat (8.3g saturated fat); 11.5g carbohydrate; 56g protein; 2.2g fibre

Sardines are available already butterflied from most fishmongers.

24 butterflied sardines (1kg)
1 clove garlic, crushed
1 tablespoon olive oil
2 tablespoons orange juice
1 teaspoon hot paprika
1 teaspoon finely chopped fresh oregano

orange and olive salad
2 medium oranges (480g)
⅓ cup (40g) seeded black olives, chopped coarsely
50g baby rocket leaves
1 fresh long red chilli, sliced thinly
1 tablespoon orange juice
½ teaspoon finely chopped fresh oregano
1 tablespoon olive oil

1 Combine ingredients in medium bowl; mix gently.
2 Make orange and olive salad.
3 Cook sardines, in batches, on heated oiled grill plate (or grill or barbecue) until browned both sides and cooked through.
4 Divide sardines among plates; serve with salad.

orange and olive salad Peel then segment oranges over medium bowl; add remaining ingredients, toss gently to combine.

did you know? Sardines are one of the heart-friendly, omega 3-rich fish that are good news for osteoporosis prevention. Sardines contain edible bones that are full of calcium and significant amounts of vitamin D.

seafood paella

preparation time 30 minutes
cooking time 1 hour 15 minutes **serves** 4
per serving 2759kJ (660 cal); 10g total fat (2.1g saturated fat); 85.4g carbohydrate; 43.2g protein; 5.4g fibre

8 uncooked large king prawns (560g)
500g small black mussels
600g squid hoods, cleaned
1 uncooked blue swimmer crab (325g)
1 tablespoon olive oil
6 green onions, chopped coarsely
2 cloves garlic, crushed
1 fresh long red chilli, chopped finely
1 medium yellow capsicum (200g), chopped coarsely
2 cups (400g) brown rice
pinch saffron threads
1 cup (250ml) dry white wine
4 medium tomatoes (600g), chopped coarsely
1 tablespoon tomato paste
1 litre (4 cups) chicken stock

1 Shell and devein prawns, leaving tails intact. Scrub mussels; remove beards. Cut squid down centre to open out; score inside in diagonal pattern then cut into thick strips.

2 To prepare crab, lift tail flap then, with a peeling motion, lift off the back shell. Remove and discard whitish gills, liver and brain matter. Rinse crab well under cold water; cut crab body in quarters.

3 Heat oil in large deep frying pan; cook onion, garlic, chilli and capsicum, stirring, until onion softens. Add rice and saffron; stir to coat in onion mixture. Stir in wine, tomato and paste. Cook, stirring, until wine has almost evaporated.

4 Add 1 cup of stock; cook, stirring, until absorbed. Add remaining stock; cook, covered, stirring occasionally, about 1 hour or until rice is tender.

5 Uncover rice; place seafood on top of the rice (do not stir to combine). Cover pan; simmer about 5 minutes or until seafood has changed in colour and mussels have opened (discard any that do not).

sushi rice

tuna cucumber mini-maki

sushi rice

preparation time 10 minutes (plus standing time)
cooking time 12 minutes **makes** 2 cups
per cup 1622kJ (388 cal); 0.5g total fat (0.1g saturated fat); 87.5g carbohydrate; 6.6g protein; 0.8g fibre

Sushi rice can be made up to 4 hours ahead. Cover; refrigerate until required.

1 cup (200g) koshihikari rice
1 cup (250ml) water
sushi vinegar
2 tablespoons rice vinegar
1 tablespoon sugar
¼ teaspoon salt

1 Place rice in large bowl, fill with cold water. Stir; drain. Repeat process until water is almost clear. Drain rice in strainer 30 minutes.
2 Meanwhile, prepare sushi vinegar.
3 Place rice and the water in medium saucepan, cover; bring to a boil. Reduce heat; simmer, covered tightly, on low heat about 12 minutes or until water is absorbed. Remove from heat; stand rice, covered, 10 minutes.
4 Place rice in large non-metallic bowl. Using large flat wooden spoon or plastic spatula, repeatedly slice through rice at sharp angles to break up lumps and separate grains.
5 Gradually add sushi vinegar. Continue to lift and turn rice with spoon, from outside to centre of bowl, about 5 minutes or until rice is almost cool. (Not all the sushi vinegar may be required; the rice should not be wet.) Cover rice with damp cloth while making sushi variations (see below and page 72 for recipes).
sushi vinegar Stir ingredients in small bowl until sugar dissolves.

tuna cucumber mini-maki

preparation time 30 minutes **makes** 48
per piece 88kJ (21 cal); 0.2g total fat (0.1g saturated fat); 3.7g carbohydrate; 1g protein; 0.2g fibre

You need a sushi or bamboo mat, available from Asian food stores and most supermarkets for this recipe.
Nori is a type of dried seaweed used in Japanese cooking as a flavouring, garnish or for sushi. It is sold in thin sheets, plain or toasted, and is available from Asian grocery stores and most supermarkets.

4 sheets toasted nori, cut in half widthways
2 cups sushi rice (see recipe above)
2 teaspoons wasabi paste
120g piece sashimi tuna, cut into 5mm strips
1 lebanese cucumber (130g), halved lengthways, seeded, cut into thin strips
¼ cup (60ml) japanese soy sauce

1 Place one nori sheet shiny-side down on sushi mat. Using damp fingers, spread ¼ cup rice over nori, leaving 2cm strip at end.
2 Dab some of the wasabi across centre of rice; layer tuna and cucumber over wasabi. Using mat, roll firmly to form sushi roll.
3 Place roll, seam-side down, on board; using sharp knife, cut roll into six mini-maki pieces.
4 Repeat with remaining nori, rice, tuna and cucumber.
5 Serve immediately with sauce, and more wasabi, if desired.
tip Wiping the knife with a damp cloth will make cutting the sushi roll easier.

inside-out rolls

preparation time 20 minutes **makes** 32
per serving 238kJ (57 cal); 0.3g total fat (0g saturated fat); 11.2g carbohydrate; 2.2g protein; 0.3g fibre

You need to make double the amount of the sushi rice for this recipe. Wiping a sharp knife with a damp cloth will make cutting the roll easier. You can use salmon roe if ocean trout roe is unavailable.

2 sheets toasted nori, cut in half widthways
4 cups sushi rice (see page 71)
2 tablespoons ocean trout roe
1 teaspoon roasted black sesame seeds
1½ tablespoons wasabi
½ lebanese cucumber (65g), halved, seeded, sliced thinly
4 cooked large king prawns (280g), shelled, deveined, halved lengthways
1 small yellow capsicum (150g), sliced thinly
2 tablespoons pink pickled ginger
¼ cup (60ml) japanese soy sauce

1 Place one nori sheet lengthways across bamboo mat about 2cm from edge of mat. Using damp fingers, spread a quarter of the rice over nori to completely cover sheet.
2 Sprinkle a quarter each of the roe and seeds over rice; cover rice completely with a piece of plastic wrap. Carefully turn mat over so nori faces up. Place back on bamboo mat, nori-side up, about 2cm from edge. Dab some wasabi across centre of nori; top with a quarter each of the cucumber, prawn, capsicum and ginger, ensuring filling extends to both ends of nori.
3 Using mat, roll firmly to form inside-out roll. Unroll mat, keeping roll in plastic wrap. Repeat with remaining ingredients.
4 Cut roll, still in plastic wrap, in half, then each half into quarters, to make eight pieces. Remove plastic wrap; serve inside-out rolls with remaining wasabi and sauce.

california handrolls

preparation time 45 minutes **makes** 40
per piece 163kJ (39 cal); 1.6g total fat (0.3g saturated fat); 5.1g carbohydrate; 0.8g protein; 0.5g fibre

⅓ cup (100g) mayonnaise
1 teaspoon wasabi paste
10 sheets toasted nori, each cut into four squares
2 cups sushi rice (see page 71)
60g cooked crab, shredded
1 lebanese cucumber (130g), seeded, sliced thinly
1 small avocado (200g), sliced thinly
1 small red capsicum (150g), sliced thinly

1 Combine mayonnaise and wasabi in small bowl.
2 Place nori, shiny-side down, diagonally across palm of hand. Using damp fingers, mould rounded teaspoons of rice into oblong shape; place across centre of seaweed. Make a slight groove down the middle of the rice for filling. Dab some of the wasabi mayonnaise along groove; top with a little crab, cucumber, avocado and capsicum.
3 Fold one side of seaweed over; fold other side of seaweed over the first to form a cone shape. Tip of cone can be folded inwards to hold shape securely.

inside-out rolls

california handrolls

salmon en papillote

ocean trout tartare

salmon en papillote

preparation time 15 minutes
cooking time 10 minutes **serves** 4
per serving 11434kJ (343 cal); 19g total fat (3.8g saturated fat); 2.6g carbohydrate; 40.1g protein; 1g fibre

Cooking something en papillote means that it is encased (in anything from baking paper to foil) so that it cooks by steaming in its own juices. In this recipe, any oily fish can be used, as long as the fillets are of equal size and thickness.

1 medium tomato (150g), seeded, chopped finely
1 tablespoon drained baby capers, rinsed
1 small red onion (100g), chopped finely
2 teaspoons finely grated lemon rind
4 x 220g salmon fillets
1 tablespoon lemon juice
1 tablespoon olive oil
80g baby rocket leaves
2 tablespoons finely shredded fresh basil

1 Preheat oven to 200°C/180°C fan-forced.
2 Combine tomato, capers, onion and rind in small bowl.
3 Place each fillet, skin-side down, on large square of oiled foil. Top each fillet with equal amounts of tomato mixture. Gather corners of square together above fish; twist to enclose securely.
4 Place parcels on oven tray; bake about 10 minutes or until fish is cooked as desired.
5 Combine lemon juice and oil in small jug. Divide rocket among serving plates.
6 Unwrap parcels just before serving; place fish on rocket. Top with basil, drizzle with oil mixture.

ocean trout tartare

preparation time 35 minutes **serves** 4
per serving 1471kJ (352 cal); 12.2g total fat (2.3g saturated fat); 23.4g carbohydrate; 34.4g protein; 3g fibre

600g piece sashimi ocean trout
2 teaspoons finely grated lemon rind
1 tablespoon lemon juice
1 tablespoon olive oil
1 clove garlic, crushed
⅓ cup finely chopped fresh flat-leaf parsley
1 medium red onion (170g), chopped finely
4 anchovy fillets, rinsed, drained, chopped finely
2 tablespoons drained baby capers, rinsed, chopped coarsely
1 small french bread stick (150g), sliced thinly
1 lemon, cut into wedges

1 Chop trout into 5mm pieces; combine in medium bowl with rind, juice, oil and garlic.
2 Divide tartare mixture among serving plates, shaping into mound. Mound equal amounts of parsley, onion, anchovy and capers around tartare mixture on plates; serve with bread slices and lemon wedges.

chicken

chicken, pea and asparagus soup with pistou

preparation time 5 minutes
cooking time 25 minutes **serves** 4
per serving 861kJ (206 cal); 5.7g total fat (1.3g saturated fat); 7.3g carbohydrate; 28.9g protein; 4.4g fibre

Pistou is a Provençal term, derived from a French word that means to pound. Similar in appearance to the Italian pesto, pistou is traditionally made with fresh herbs, olive oil and garlic. You need 450g of fresh peas in the pod or 2 cups (240g) frozen peas for this recipe.

3 cups (750ml) chicken stock
3 cups (750ml) water
1 clove garlic, crushed
¼ teaspoon coarsely ground black pepper
400g chicken breast fillets
170g asparagus, trimmed, chopped coarsely
1½ cups (240g) shelled fresh peas
1 tablespoon lemon juice

pistou

½ cup coarsely chopped fresh flat-leaf parsley
½ cup coarsely chopped fresh mint
¼ cup coarsely chopped fresh garlic chives
2 teaspoons finely grated lemon rind
1 clove garlic, crushed
2 teaspoons olive oil

1 Bring stock, the water, garlic and pepper to a boil in large saucepan. Add chicken; return to boil. Reduce heat; simmer, covered, about 10 minutes or until chicken is cooked through. Cool in poaching liquid 10 minutes. Remove chicken from pan; slice thinly.
2 Meanwhile, make pistou.
3 Add remaining ingredients to soup; bring to a boil. Return chicken to pan; simmer, uncovered, about 3 minutes or until vegetables are just tender.
4 Divide soup among serving bowls; top with pistou.
pistou Using mortar and pestle, pound ingredients until smooth.

did you know? Adequate protein is essential for muscle repair and maintenance. However, a gram of dietary protein is not converted to a gram of muscle. If you want to increase your muscle mass you need to combine a well-balanced diet with an appropriate strength-training program.

kofta with date chutney and spiced eggplant

preparation time 30 minutes (plus refrigeration time)
cooking time 45 minutes **serves** 4
per serving 1935kJ (463 cal); 17.8g total fat (3.5g saturated fat); 37.1g carbohydrate; 35.4g protein; 8.6g fibre

¼ cup (50g) brown rice
1 tablespoon olive oil
1 small brown onion (80g), chopped finely
1 clove garlic, crushed
1 long green chilli, chopped finely
500g chicken mince
½ cup firmly packed fresh coriander leaves
1 egg

spiced eggplant
1 tablespoon olive oil
2 teaspoons cumin seeds
2 teaspoons yellow mustard seeds
6 baby eggplants (360g), sliced thickly
1 medium brown onion (150g), sliced thinly
1 clove garlic, crushed
½ cup (125ml) water
420g can chickpeas, rinsed, drained
¼ cup firmly packed fresh coriander leaves

date chutney
½ cup (70g) seeded dried dates, chopped finely
¼ cup (60ml) orange juice
¼ cup (60ml) water

1 Cook rice in large saucepan of boiling water, uncovered, until just tender; drain. Rinse under cold water; drain.
2 Heat oil in small frying pan; cook onion, garlic and chilli, stirring, until onion softens. Process onion mixture with chicken, rice, coriander and egg until smooth.
3 Shape chicken mixture into 12 patties. Place patties on tray, cover; refrigerate until required.
4 Make spiced eggplant. Make date chutney.
5 Cook kofta patties on heated oiled grill plate (or grill or barbecue) until browned both sides and cooked through. Serve kofta with eggplant; top with date chutney.

spiced eggplant Heat oil in medium saucepan; fry seeds over low heat until fragrant. Add eggplant, onion and garlic; cook, stirring, about 5 minutes or until just softened. Add the water and chickpeas; bring to a boil. Reduce heat; simmer, uncovered, about 15 minutes or until mixture thickens. Remove from heat; cool 10 minutes then stir in coriander.

date chutney Combine ingredients in small saucepan; bring to a boil. Reduce heat; simmer, uncovered, 5 minutes. Cool 5 minutes; blend or process until smooth.

pepita sesame cutlets with mint and parsley salad

preparation time 20 minutes (plus refrigeration time)
cooking time 50 minutes **serves** 4
per serving 1542kJ (369 cal); 21.9g total fat (4g saturated fat); 2g carbohydrate; 28.8g protein; 4.5g fibre

1 tablespoon sesame seeds
⅓ cup (65g) pepitas
2 teaspoons finely grated lime rind
2 tablespoons lime juice
2 cloves garlic, crushed
4 chicken thigh cutlets (800g)
1 egg white, beaten lightly

mint and parsley salad

1 tablespoon macadamia oil
2 tablespoons lime juice
1 tablespoon apple cider vinegar
1 cup firmly packed fresh flat-leaf parsley leaves
1 cup firmly packed fresh mint leaves
125g cherry tomatoes, halved
2 green onions, sliced thinly

1 Preheat oven to 200°C/180°C fan-forced.
2 Combine seeds, pepitas, rind, juice and garlic in small bowl.
3 Brush chicken all over with egg white; press seed mixture onto top side only. Refrigerate chicken on oven tray, seeded-side up, 10 minutes. Cook, covered, 30 minutes. Uncover, cook 20 minutes.
4 Meanwhile, make mint and parsley salad. Serve chicken with salad.

mint and parsley salad Whisk oil, juice and vinegar in medium bowl. Add remaining ingredients; toss gently to combine.

chicken, mixed vegies and almond stir-fry

preparation time 15 minutes
cooking time 20 minutes **serves** 4
per serving 3515kJ (841 cal); 20.2g total fat (3.1g saturated fat); 109.4g carbohydrate; 50.5g protein; 7.5g fibre

2½ cups (500g) jasmine rice
2 tablespoons peanut oil
600g chicken breast fillets, sliced thinly
1 medium brown onion (150g), sliced thinly
2 cloves garlic, crushed
350g broccolini, trimmed, chopped coarsely
115g fresh baby corn, halved lengthways
150g sugar snap peas, trimmed
⅓ cup (45g) roasted slivered almonds
1 tablespoon fish sauce
1 tablespoon sweet chilli sauce

1 Cook rice in large saucepan of boiling water, uncovered, until just tender; drain. Cover to keep warm.
2 Meanwhile, heat half the oil in wok; stir-fry chicken, in batches, until browned lightly and cooked through.
3 Heat remaining oil in wok; stir-fry onion and garlic until onion softens. Add broccolini, corn and peas; stir-fry until vegetables are tender.
4 Return chicken to wok with nuts and sauces; stir-fry until heated through. Serve with rice.

pepita sesame cutlets with mint and parsley salad

chicken, mixed vegies and almond stir-fry

did you know? Over recent years, serving sizes have been getting larger and larger – nowadays, one serve of ice-cream or one bottle of drink can be several times larger than the portion sizes of the past. Be aware of portion distortion at home, too, such as when you're plating out evening meals. Aim to keep serving sizes modest and don't overeat.

oven-baked drumsticks with soy bean salad

preparation time 25 minutes (plus standing time)
cooking time 1 hour 20 minutes **serves** 4
per serving 2002kJ (479 cal); 22.3g total fat (4.9g saturated fat); 14.7g carbohydrate; 48.1g protein; 11.3g fibre

½ cup (100g) dried soy beans
1 tablespoon olive oil
1 tablespoon finely grated lemon rind
1 tablespoon finely chopped fresh oregano
8 chicken drumsticks (1.2kg)
1 cup loosely packed fresh flat-leaf parsley leaves
½ cup loosely packed fresh basil leaves
½ cup loosely packed fresh oregano leaves
½ small red onion (50g), sliced thinly
2 tablespoons lemon juice
1 clove garlic, crushed

sun-dried tomato coulis

1 medium brown onion (150g), chopped finely
4 medium tomatoes (600g), chopped coarsely
½ cup (140g) tomato paste
¼ cup drained sun-dried tomatoes in oil, chopped finely

1 Cover beans with cold water in medium bowl; stand overnight. Drain beans, rinse under cold water; drain. Place beans in medium saucepan of boiling water; return to a boil. Reduce heat; simmer, uncovered, about 30 minutes or until beans are almost tender. Drain.

2 Preheat oven to 200°C/180°C fan-forced.

3 Combine oil, rind and chopped oregano in large bowl. Remove and discard skin from drumsticks. Add drumsticks to bowl; turn to coat in oregano mixture.

4 Place drumsticks, in single layer, in oiled shallow baking dish, cover with foil; bake, turning half-way through cooking, about 50 minutes or until cooked through.

5 Meanwhile, make sun-dried tomato coulis.

6 Combine cooled beans in medium bowl with remaining herbs, onion, juice and garlic.

7 Serve chicken, topped with coulis, with bean salad.

sun-dried tomato coulis Heat oiled medium saucepan; cook onion, tomato and paste, covered, over low heat about 20 minutes. Blend or process until smooth. Push mixture through sieve into medium bowl; discard solids. Stir in sun-dried tomato.

italian white bean and chicken stew

preparation time 35 minutes
(plus standing time)
cooking time 35 minutes **serves** 4
per serving 2119kJ (507 cal); 23.3g total fat (6.2g saturated fat); 16.2g carbohydrate; 54.5g protein; 9g fibre

1 cup (200g) dried cannellini beans
1kg chicken thigh fillets, chopped coarsely
¼ cup finely chopped fresh oregano
1 tablespoon olive oil
1 medium fennel bulb (300g)
2 medium brown onions (300g), sliced thinly
2 cloves garlic, crushed
6 medium tomatoes (900g), peeled, seeded, chopped coarsely
3 large zucchini (450g), chopped coarsely
½ cup coarsely chopped fresh basil

1 Cover beans with cold water in medium bowl; stand overnight. Drain beans; rinse under cold water, drain. Place beans in medium saucepan of boiling water; return to a boil. Reduce heat; simmer, uncovered, about 30 minutes or until beans are almost tender. Drain.

2 Meanwhile, combine chicken and oregano in medium bowl. Heat oil in large saucepan; cook chicken, in batches, until browned.

3 Trim then slice fennel thinly. Coarsely chop enough fennel fronds to make 2 tablespoons; reserve.

4 Cook onion, garlic and sliced fennel in same dish, stirring, until vegetables just soften. Return chicken to dish with tomato, zucchini and beans; cook, covered, over low heat, about 15 minutes or until chicken is cooked through. Uncover; simmer 5 minutes.

5 Remove stew from heat; stir in basil and reserved fronds. Serve stew with a loaf of french bread, if desired.

did you know? Family meals are vitally important to help your kids get a healthy start. Smorgasbord or platter style (rather than plated) works best, so children can choose what they like and how much they need. Remember, children usually have a very good sense of how much or how little food they need, but this ability is lost as they get older and become more accustomed to serving sizes.

harissa-roasted chicken and veg

preparation time 35 minutes (plus standing time)
cooking time 2 hours **serves** 4
per serving 2717kJ (650 cal); 37.5g total fat (10.7g saturated fat); 27.9g carbohydrate; 46.1g protein; 8.3g fibre

1 small orange (180g), cut into thin wedges
1.6kg chicken
1 tablespoon olive oil
300g baby onions
500g baby new potatoes
1 bulb garlic, separated into cloves
4 baby eggplants (240g), halved lengthways
250g cherry tomatoes

harissa

⅓ cup (15g) dried red chillies, chopped coarsely
½ teaspoon ground cumin
½ teaspoon ground coriander
½ teaspoon caraway seeds
1 clove garlic, quartered
1 tablespoon tomato paste
2 teaspoons finely grated orange rind
¼ cup (60ml) orange juice

1 Make harissa.

2 Preheat oven to 180°C/160°C fan-forced.

3 Place orange inside cavity of chicken. Make a pocket between breast and skin with fingers; rub 2 tablespoons of the harissa under skin inside pocket. Tie legs together with kitchen string; brush chicken all over with 2 tablespoons of the harissa.

4 Half-fill large shallow baking dish with water; place chicken on oiled wire rack over dish. Roast, uncovered, about 1 hour.

5 Meanwhile, heat oil in large flameproof baking dish; cook onions, potatoes and unpeeled garlic, stirring, until vegetables are browned.

6 Cover chicken; roast about 50 minutes or until chicken is cooked through. Add eggplant and tomatoes to vegetable mixture in dish; place in oven for about the last 20 minutes of chicken cooking time or until vegetables are tender.

7 Serve chicken with roasted vegetables and remaining harissa.

harissa Place chilli in small heatproof bowl, cover with boiling water; stand 1 hour. Drain chilli; reserve ¼ cup soaking liquid. Dry-fry cumin, coriander and caraway in small heated frying pan until fragrant. Blend or process spices with chilli, reserved soaking liquid, garlic and paste until mixture is smooth; transfer harissa to small bowl, stir in rind and juice.

poached chicken in citrus wakame broth

preparation time 25 minutes
cooking time 25 minutes **serves** 4
per serving 1053kJ (252 cal); 3.9g total fat (1.2g saturated fat); 20.9g carbohydrate; 30.7g protein; 3.3g fibre

Wakame is a highly nutritious seaweed that is black when purchased dried, but reconstitutes to a bright-green colour. The leaves are usually stripped from the central vein.

5g dried wakame
3cm piece fresh ginger (15g), sliced thinly
1 fresh small red thai chilli, sliced thinly
2 cloves garlic, sliced thinly
2 kaffir lime leaves, torn
1 litre (4 cups) chicken stock
2 cups (500ml) water
2 chicken breast fillets (400g)
100g dried soba noodles
½ cup (40g) bean sprouts
2 tablespoons fish sauce
⅓ cup (80ml) lime juice
2 baby buk choy (300g), leaves separated

1 Place wakame in small bowl, cover with cold water; stand about 10 minutes or until softened. Drain then squeeze out excess water. Chop coarsely, removing any hard ribs or stems.

2 Combine ginger, chilli, garlic, lime leaves, stock, the water and chicken in large saucepan; bring to a boil. Reduce heat; simmer, uncovered, about 10 minutes or until cooked through. Cool chicken in broth 10 minutes; remove from pan. Strain broth through muslin-lined sieve over large bowl; discard solids, return broth to pan. Slice chicken thinly.

3 Meanwhile, cook noodles in large saucepan of boiling water, uncovered, until just tender; drain. Divide noodles, wakame and sprouts among serving bowls.

4 Bring broth to a boil; reduce heat and stir in sauce, juice and buk choy. Serve broth topped with chicken, and accompanied with lime wedges, if desired.

meat

moussaka stacks

preparation time 25 minutes
cooking time 30 minutes serves 4
per serving 1973kJ (472 cal); 30.2g total fat (13.2g saturated fat); 7.8g carbohydrate; 40.5g protein; 3.5g fibre

2 tablespoons olive oil
1 medium brown onion (150g), chopped finely
2 cloves garlic, crushed
500g beef mince
¼ teaspoon ground cinnamon
½ teaspoon ground nutmeg
2 teaspoons finely grated lemon rind
1 cup (250ml) beef stock
200g fetta cheese, crumbled
½ cup coarsely chopped fresh flat-leaf parsley
1 medium eggplant (300g)
2 medium egg tomatoes (150g), sliced lengthways
20g baby spinach leaves

yogurt dressing
⅔ cup (190g) yogurt
1 tablespoon water
2 teaspoons finely chopped preserved lemon

1 Heat oil in large frying pan; cook onion and garlic, stirring, until onion softens. Add beef, spices and rind; cook, stirring, until beef is cooked through.
2 Add stock, bring to a boil. Reduce heat; simmer, uncovered, about 15 minutes or until liquid is absorbed. Remove from heat; stir in cheese and parsley.
3 Meanwhile, make yogurt dressing.
4 Slice eggplant into 10 slices lengthways; discard two skin-side pieces. Cook eggplant and tomato, in batches, on heated oiled grill plate (or grill or barbecue) until browned lightly both sides and tender.
5 Divide half the beef mixture among serving plates, top each with a slice of eggplant, tomato then some of the spinach; drizzle half the dressing over stacks. Repeat making each stack with the remaining ingredients; serve sprinkled with extra parsley leaves, if desired.

yogurt dressing Combine ingredients in small bowl.

mexican shredded beef soup

preparation time 20 minutes
cooking time 2 hours 20 minutes **serves** 4
per serving 1413kJ (338 cal); 9g total fat (2g saturated fat); 25.9g carbohydrate; 34.3g protein; 7.4g fibre

500g piece beef skirt steak
2 litres (8 cups) water
1 bay leaf
6 black peppercorns
1 large carrot (180g), chopped coarsely
1 trimmed celery stalk (100g), chopped coarsely
1 tablespoon olive oil
1 medium brown onion (150g), sliced thickly
1 medium red capsicum (200g), sliced thickly
1 medium green capsicum (200g), sliced thickly
2 cloves garlic, crushed
2 fresh long red chillies, chopped finely
1 teaspoon ground cumin
400g can crushed tomatoes
⅓ cup loosely packed fresh oregano leaves
1 trimmed corn cob (250g)
4 corn tortillas

1 Tie beef with kitchen string at 3cm intervals. Place in large saucepan with the water, bay leaf, peppercorns, carrot and celery; bring to a boil. Reduce heat; simmer, covered, 1½ hours. Uncover; simmer about 30 minutes or until beef is tender.

2 Cool beef in stock 10 minutes. Transfer beef to large bowl; using two forks, shred beef coarsely. Strain stock through muslin-lined sieve over another large bowl; discard solids, return stock to pan.

3 Heat oil in medium frying pan; cook onion, capsicums, garlic, chilli and cumin, stirring, until vegetables soften. Add onion mixture, beef, undrained tomatoes and ¼ cup of the oregano to pan with stock; bring to a boil. Reduce heat; simmer, uncovered, 10 minutes.

4 Cut corn kernels from cob. Add corn to soup; cook, uncovered, until just tender.

5 Meanwhile, preheat grill. Just before serving, cut each tortilla into 8 wedges; place on oven tray, in single layer, toast until crisp. Sprinkle remaining oregano over soup, serve with tortillas.

slow-cooked thai lamb shanks

preparation time 30 minutes
cooking time 2 hours 15 minutes **serves** 4
per serving 1492kJ (357 cal); 12.5g total fat (5.6g saturated fat); 11.7g carbohydrate; 48.1g protein; 2.6g fibre

2 star anise
2 teaspoons ground coriander
⅓ cup (100g) tamarind concentrate
2 tablespoons brown sugar
8cm piece fresh ginger (40g), sliced thinly
1 fresh small red thai chilli, sliced thinly
2 cloves garlic, sliced thinly
1 tablespoon kecap manis
1 cup (250ml) water
8 french-trimmed lamb shanks (2kg)
500g choy sum, chopped into 10cm lengths

1 Preheat oven to 180°C/160°C fan-forced.

2 Dry-fry star anise and coriander in small heated frying pan, stirring, until fragrant. Combine spices with tamarind, sugar, ginger, chilli, garlic, kecap manis and the water in medium jug.

3 Place lamb, in single layer, in large shallow baking dish; drizzle with tamarind mixture. Cook, covered, turning lamb occasionally, about 2 hours or until meat is almost falling off the bone.

4 Remove lamb from dish; cover to keep warm. Skim away excess fat from pan juices then strain into small saucepan. Bring sauce to a boil; boil, uncovered, 5 minutes.

5 Steam choy sum until just tender then divide among serving plates. Top with lamb; drizzle with sauce.

mushroom, beef and barley casserole

preparation time 15 minutes
cooking time 3 hours **serves** 4
per serving 2851kJ (682 cal); 22.4g total fat (6.3g saturated fat); 43g carbohydrate; 60.5g protein; 11.5g fibre

2 tablespoons olive oil
1kg beef chuck steak, diced into 3cm cubes
8 pickling onions (320g), halved
2 medium carrots (240g), chopped coarsely
1 cup (250ml) dry red wine
1 cup (250ml) beef stock
2 x 400g cans diced tomatoes
2 sprigs fresh rosemary
7 black peppercorns
200g button mushrooms
½ cup (100g) pearl barley
2 tablespoons fresh oregano leaves

1 Preheat oven to 180°C/160°C fan-forced.

2 Heat half the oil in large flameproof casserole dish; cook beef, in batches, until browned.

3 Heat remaining oil in same dish; cook onion and carrot, stirring, until vegetables soften. Return beef to dish with wine, stock, undrained tomatoes, rosemary and peppercorns; bring to a boil. Cover; cook in oven 2 hours, stirring occasionally.

4 Stir in mushrooms and barley, return to oven; cook, uncovered, 45 minutes or until barley is tender. Serve sprinkled with oregano.

slow-cooked thai lamb shanks

mushroom, beef and barley casserole

did you know? Red meat is an often-neglected food in the female diet. In fact, Australian women have decreased their red meat intake by 25 per cent over the last five years. A medium serve of lean red meat can give you approximately one third of your daily iron requirements.

kashmiri lamb with spicy dhal

preparation time 30 minutes (plus standing and refrigeration time) **cooking time** 1 hour 15 minutes **serves** 4
per serving 2625kJ (628 cal); 23.2g total fat (4.7g saturated fat); 44.5g carbohydrate; 54.2g protein; 12.9g fibre

1 teaspoon hot paprika
2 teaspoons ground coriander
2 teaspoons ground cumin
¼ cup (60ml) vegetable oil
600g lamb backstraps
1 cup (200g) dried chickpeas
1 cup (200g) yellow split peas
1 medium brown onion (150g), chopped finely
2 cloves garlic, crushed
2cm piece fresh ginger (10g), grated
½ teaspoon ground turmeric
1 teaspoon garam masala
1 teaspoon ground chilli
2 medium tomatoes (300g), chopped coarsely
3 cups (750ml) water
½ cup coarsely chopped fresh coriander leaves

1 Cover chickpeas and split peas with cold water in large bowl. Soak overnight; rinse, drain.
2 Combine paprika, half the ground coriander, half the cumin, 1 tablespoon of the oil and lamb in large bowl. Cover, refrigerate 3 hours or overnight.
3 Heat 1 tablespoon of the remaining oil in large saucepan; cook onion, garlic and ginger, stirring, until onion softens. Stir in remaining ground coriander and cumin, turmeric, garam masala and chilli; cook, stirring, until fragrant.
4 Add peas, tomato and the water; bring to a boil. Reduce heat; simmer, covered, stirring occasionally, about 1 hour or until dhal is tender. Remove from heat; stir in fresh coriander.
5 Meanwhile, heat remaining oil in large frying pan; cook lamb, uncovered, until browned and cooked as desired. Cover; stand 10 minutes then slice thickly. Serve with dhal, and yogurt, if desired.

did you know? Iron is very important for maximising energy levels and it also plays a vital role in immune function. Not getting enough dietary iron can leave you feeling tired and wrung-out, and increase the likelihood of illness. Lean red meat is one of the best sources of readily absorbable haem iron (iron sources from meat). Beef and lamb are also great sources of zinc and many of the B vitamins, especially vitamin B12.

glazed pork and watercress salad

preparation time 15 minutes
cooking time 15 minutes **serves** 4
per serving 1885kJ (451 cal); 14.1g total fat (3.2g saturated fat); 29.9g carbohydrate; 49.6g protein; 4.3g fibre

¼ cup (90g) honey
¼ cup (85g) tamarind concentrate
3cm piece fresh ginger (15g), grated
2 cloves garlic, crushed
800g pork fillets
100g watercress, trimmed
1 medium red onion (170g), sliced thinly
2 lebanese cucumbers (260g), seeded, sliced thinly
1 medium yellow capsicum (200g), sliced thinly
½ cup (75g) roasted unsalted cashews

1 Combine honey, tamarind, ginger and garlic in small jug. Combine pork with a third of the honey mixture in medium bowl.
2 Cook pork on heated oiled grill plate (or grill or barbecue) until browned all over and cooked as desired. Cover; stand 10 minutes then slice thickly.
3 Meanwhile, combine remaining ingredients with half the remaining honey mixture in medium bowl.
4 Drizzle pork with remaining honey mixture; serve with salad.

lemon chilli pork with italian brown rice salad

preparation time 35 minutes
cooking time 50 minutes **serves** 4
per serving 1969kJ (471 cal); 14.7g total fat (2.9g saturated fat); 46.4g carbohydrate; 35.7g protein; 3g fibre

2 teaspoons finely grated lemon rind
2 tablespoons lemon juice
½ teaspoon dried chilli flakes
1 tablespoon olive oil
4 x 240g pork cutlets

italian brown rice salad
1 cup (200g) brown long-grain rice
1 medium red capsicum (200g), chopped finely
½ cup (60g) seeded black olives, chopped coarsely
2 tablespoons drained capers, rinsed
½ cup coarsely chopped fresh basil
⅓ cup coarsely chopped fresh flat-leaf parsley
2 tablespoons lemon juice
1 tablespoon olive oil

1 Combine rind, juice, chilli, oil and pork in medium bowl. Cover; refrigerate until required.
2 Make italian brown rice salad.
3 Cook pork, uncovered, in large heated frying pan about 15 minutes or until cooked as desired. Serve with rice salad.

italian brown rice salad Cook rice in large saucepan of boiling water, uncovered, until tender; drain. Rinse under cold water; drain. Combine rice in large bowl with remaining ingredients.

glazed pork and watercress salad

lemon chilli pork with italian brown rice salad

spinach, tomato and prosciutto wholegrain pizza

preparation time 25 minutes (plus standing time)
cooking time 15 minutes **serves** 6
per serving 1547kJ (370 cal); 6.5g total fat (3g saturated fat); 55.7g carbohydrate; 18g protein; 7.4g fibre

- ⅓ cup (55g) finely cracked buckwheat
- ¼ cup (40g) burghul
- 1 cup (250ml) warm water
- 1 teaspoon caster sugar
- 8g sachet dried yeast
- 1½ cups (225g) plain flour
- 1 cup (160g) wholemeal plain flour
- ⅔ cup (170g) bottled tomato pasta sauce
- 1 cup (100g) coarsely grated mozzarella cheese
- 80g baby spinach leaves, trimmed
- 250g grape tomatoes, halved
- 8 slices prosciutto (120g), chopped coarsely

1 Combine buckwheat and burghul in medium heatproof bowl; cover with boiling water. Cover; stand 30 minutes. Rinse under cold water; drain thoroughly.

2 Combine the warm water, sugar and yeast in small jug. Stand in warm place about 10 minutes or until frothy.

3 Combine buckwheat mixture in large bowl with flours. Add yeast mixture; mix to a soft dough. Knead dough on floured surface about 10 minutes or until smooth and elastic. Place dough in lightly greased large bowl; cover. Stand in warm place about 1 hour or until doubled in size.

4 Preheat oven to 220°C/200°C fan-forced; grease two pizza trays or oven trays.

5 Divide dough in half. Roll each portion on floured surface into 30cm round; place one on each tray.

6 Spread pizza bases with sauce; sprinkle with half the cheese then top with spinach, tomato and prosciutto; sprinkle pizzas with remaining cheese. Bake, uncovered, about 20 minutes or until top is browned lightly and bases are crisp.

fruit

berry-muesli baked apples

preparation time 25 minutes
cooking time 45 minutes **serves** 4
per serving 681kJ (163 cal); 5.4g total fat (2.9g saturated fat); 26g carbohydrate; 1.4g protein; 4.4g fibre

4 large granny smith apples (800g)
cooking-oil spray
⅓ cup (35g) natural muesli
½ cup (75g) fresh blueberries
20g butter, melted
3 teaspoons brown sugar

1 Preheat oven to 160°C/140°C fan-forced.
2 Core unpeeled apples about three-quarters of the way down from stem end, making hole 4cm in diameter. Use small sharp knife to score around circumference of each apple; lightly spray each apple with cooking oil.
3 Combine remaining ingredients in small bowl. Divide mixture among apples, pressing firmly into holes; place apples in small baking dish. Bake, uncovered, about 45 minutes or until apples are just softened.

did you know? In the nutrition stakes, fruit is way up at the top of the list. As a group, fruit makes a significant contribution to our carbohydrate, dietary fibre, vitamin C, beta-carotene, folate and potassium intakes. That's why the government is promoting greater fruit and vegetable consumption in the "Go for 2 & 5" (2 fruit and 5 vegetables daily) campaign.

clockwise from top: lime sorbet,
blood orange sorbet, grapefruit sorbet

lime sorbet

preparation time 20 minutes
cooking time 10 minutes (plus cooling and freezing time) **serves** 8
per serving 472kJ (113 cal); 0.1g total fat (0g saturated fat); 27.9g carbohydrate; 0.7g protein; 0.2g fibre

2 tablespoons finely grated lime rind
1 cup (220g) caster sugar
2½ cups (625ml) water
¾ cup (180ml) lime juice
1 egg white

1 Stir rind, sugar and water in medium saucepan over high heat until sugar dissolves; bring to a boil. Reduce heat; simmer without stirring, uncovered, 5 minutes. Transfer to large heatproof jug, cool to room temperature; stir in juice.
2 Pour sorbet mixture into loaf pan; cover tightly with foil; freeze 3 hours or overnight.
3 Process mixture with egg white until smooth. Return to loaf pan, cover; freeze until firm. Serve sprinkled with extra lime rind, if desired.

grapefruit sorbet

preparation time 20 minutes
cooking time 10 minutes (plus cooling and freezing time) **serves** 8
per serving 481kJ (115 cal); 0g total fat (0g saturated fat); 29.3g carbohydrate; 0.6g protein; 0.1g fibre

2 tablespoons finely grated ruby grapefruit rind
1 cup (220g) caster sugar
2½ cups (625ml) water
¾ cup (180ml) ruby red grapefruit juice
1 egg white

1 Stir rind, sugar and water in medium saucepan over high heat until sugar dissolves; bring to a boil. Reduce heat; simmer without stirring, uncovered, 5 minutes. Transfer to large heatproof jug, cool to room temperature; stir in juice.
2 Pour sorbet mixture into loaf pan; cover tightly with foil; freeze 3 hours or overnight.
3 Process mixture with egg white until smooth. Return to loaf pan, cover; freeze until firm. Serve sprinkled with extra grapefruit rind, if desired.

blood orange sorbet

preparation time 20 minutes
cooking time 10 minutes (plus cooling and freezing time) **serves** 8
per serving 497kJ (119 cal); 0g total fat (0g saturated fat); 30.2g carbohydrate; 0.6g protein; 0.1g fibre

2 tablespoons finely grated blood orange rind
1 cup (220g) caster sugar
2½ cups (625ml) water
1 cup (250ml) blood orange juice
1 egg white

1 Stir rind, sugar and water in medium saucepan over high heat until sugar dissolves; bring to a boil. Reduce heat; simmer without stirring, uncovered, 5 minutes. Transfer to large heatproof jug, cool to room temperature; stir in juice.
2 Pour sorbet mixture into loaf pan; cover tightly with foil; freeze 3 hours or overnight.
3 Process mixture with egg white until smooth. Return to loaf pan, cover; freeze until firm. Serve sprinkled with extra orange rind, if desired.

pear, rhubarb and ricotta tarts

preparation time 15 minutes
cooking time 25 minutes
(plus refrigeration time) **makes** 4
per serving 803kJ (192 cal); 8.3g total fat (4.4g saturated fat); 21.2g carbohydrate; 8.5g protein; 1.4g fibre

You need 1 large trimmed stalk of rhubarb for the tart filling.

- 1¼ cups (250g) low-fat ricotta cheese
- 2 egg yolks
- 2 tablespoons caster sugar
- 2 teaspoons plain flour
- ½ cup (55g) finely chopped fresh rhubarb
- 1 small pear (180g), quartered, sliced thinly lengthways
- 1 tablespoon caster sugar, extra

1 Preheat oven to 200°C/180°C fan-forced. Grease four 10cm-round deep fluted tins; place on oven tray.

2 Beat ricotta, egg yolks, sugar and flour in small bowl with electric mixer until smooth; stir in rhubarb.

3 Spread mixture into tins; top each with pear, sprinkle with extra sugar. Bake about 25 minutes or until filling sets. Cool 10 minutes, cover; refrigerate until cold.

plum and apple crumble

preparation time 15 minutes
cooking time 45 minutes **serves** 6
per serving 1810kJ (433 cal); 24.8g total fat (2.4g saturated fat); 31.2g carbohydrate; 8.6g protein; 7.4g fibre

- 4 medium blood plums (450g), cut into thin wedges
- 2 tablespoons lemon juice
- 2 tablespoons water
- 4 medium apples (600g), cut into thin wedges
- 1 tablespoon honey

crumble topping

- ½ cup (45g) rolled oats
- ½ cup (100g) pepitas
- ½ cup (75g) sunflower seed kernels
- ½ cup (70g) coarsely chopped roasted hazelnuts
- 2 tablespoons honey
- 1 tablespoon walnut oil

ricotta cream

- ⅔ cup (130g) low-fat ricotta cheese
- 1 teaspoon ground cinnamon
- 2 tablespoons low-fat milk

1 Preheat oven to 180°C/160°C fan-forced. Grease six 1¼-cup (310ml) ovenproof dishes.

2 Combine plum, half the juice and half the water in medium saucepan; cook over low heat, stirring occasionally, 10 minutes.

3 Combine apple, remaining juice and the remaining water in another medium saucepan; cook over low heat, stirring occasionally, 5 minutes. Combine plum and apple mixtures in medium bowl with honey.

4 Meanwhile, make crumble topping. Make ricotta cream.

5 Divide fruit mixture among dishes; sprinkle with crumble mixture. Bake about 30 minutes or until golden brown; serve with ricotta cream.

crumble topping Combine ingredients in small bowl.

ricotta cream Combine ingredients in small deep bowl; beat with electric mixer until smooth.

pear, rhubarb and ricotta tarts

plum and apple crumble

did you know? You can't go wrong with including more fruit in your diet. While the official recommendations are at least 2-4 servings a day for Australian adults, and 5 during pregnancy, research suggests that we would all benefit from more servings.

pineapple and kiwifruit salad in basil lemon syrup

preparation time 20 minutes (plus refrigeration time)
cooking time 20 minutes serves 4
per serving 627kJ (150 cal); 0.5g total fat (0g saturated fat); 26.6g carbohydrate; 3.6g protein; 9g fibre

You need 4 large passionfruit for this recipe.

1½ cups (375ml) water
2 x 5cm strips lemon rind
½ cup (125ml) lemon juice
1 tablespoon caster sugar
¼ cup firmly packed fresh basil leaves
1 small pineapple (900g), quartered, sliced thinly
6 medium kiwifruit (510g), sliced thinly
⅓ cup (80ml) passionfruit pulp
1 tablespoon finely shredded fresh basil

1 Combine the water, rind, juice, sugar and basil leaves in medium frying pan; bring to a boil. Reduce heat; simmer, uncovered, 20 minutes. Strain syrup into medium jug; discard rind and basil. Cool 10 minutes; refrigerate.
2 Just before serving, combine syrup in large bowl with remaining ingredients.

frozen mango parfait

preparation time 20 minutes (plus freezing time) serves 12
per serving 986kJ (236 cal); 12.3g total fat (8g saturated fat); 27.4g carbohydrate; 4.7g protein; 1.2g fibre

1 medium mango (430g), chopped coarsely
2 cups (440g) low-fat ricotta cheese
¾ cup (165g) caster sugar
300ml light thickened cream

tropical fruit salsa
¼ cup (55g) caster sugar
¼ cup (60ml) water
2 medium kiwifruit (170g), chopped coarsely
1 medium mango (430g), chopped coarsely
2 kaffir lime leaves, sliced thinly

1 Line base of 14cm x 21cm loaf pan with foil, extending 5cm over edges.
2 Blend or process mango until smooth.
3 Beat ricotta and sugar in small bowl with electric mixer until smooth; transfer mixture to large bowl. Beat cream in small bowl with electric mixer until soft peaks form; fold cream into ricotta mixture.
4 Drop alternate spoonfuls of ricotta mixture and mango pulp into pan. Pull skewer backwards and forwards through parfait mixture several times for marbled effect; smooth surface with spatula. Cover with foil; freeze overnight.
5 Make tropical fruit salsa 1 hour before serving. Cover, refrigerate until cold. Serve parfait topped with salsa.
tropical fruit salsa Combine sugar and the water in small saucepan; bring to a boil. Reduce heat; simmer, uncovered, without stirring, 5 minutes; cool. Combine sugar syrup with remaining ingredients in medium bowl.

pineapple and kiwifruit salad in basil lemon syrup

frozen mango parfait

did you know? Recently, UK researchers found an ingredient in chocolate, theobromine, was nearly a third more effective in stopping coughing than the pharmaceutical of choice, codeine. Theobromine appears to work like standard cough treatments, suppressing nerve activity that causes coughing.

herbal & spiced teas

did you know? There have been some reports that caffeine intake from tea and coffee may reduce bone mineral density (a risk factor for osteoporosis), however, adding milk to regular tea or coffee is thought to counteract this.

chai tea

preparation time 10 minutes (plus refrigeration time) **serves** 8
per serving 113kJ (27 cal); 0.6g total fat (0.4g saturated fat); 5g carbohydrate; 0.5g protein; 0g fibre

Keep leftover spiced milk mixture, covered, under refrigeration for up to five days.

2 teaspoons honey
1 teaspoon ground cardamom
½ teaspoon ground cinnamon
½ teaspoon ground clove
½ teaspoon ground ginger
395g can sweetened condensed milk
8 english breakfast tea bags
1.25 litres (5 cups) boiling water

1 Combine honey, spices and milk in small bowl. Cover; refrigerate 3 hours or overnight.
2 Place one teabag in each cup or tea glass. Add the boiling water; stand 3 minutes. Discard tea bag; stir 1 teaspoon of spiced milk into each serving.

mint, ginger and lemon grass tea

preparation time 5 minutes
cooking time 5 minutes **serves** 4
per serving 84kJ (20 cal); 0.1g total fat (0g saturated fat); 4g carbohydrate; 0.3g protein; 0.8g fibre

10cm stick fresh lemon grass (20g), chopped coarsely
10cm piece fresh ginger (50g), chopped coarsely
½ cup loosely packed fresh mint leaves
1 tablespoon grated palm sugar
1 litre (4 cups) water

1 Combine ingredients in small saucepan; bring to a boil. Simmer, uncovered, 5 minutes.
2 Stand 5 minutes; strain into large heatproof jug.

rosemary mint camomile tea

preparation time 5 minutes **serves** 4
per serving 105kJ (25 cal); 0g total fat (0g saturated fat); 6.1g carbohydrate; 0.1g protein; 0.3g fibre

5cm piece fresh rosemary
¼ cup loosely packed fresh peppermint leaves
4 camomile tea bags
5cm strip lemon rind
1 tablespoon honey
1 litre (4 cups) boiling water

1 Combine ingredients in large heatproof jug; stand 3 minutes before straining into cups or tea glasses.

lemon balm and mint cooler

preparation time 15 minutes
cooking time 10 minutes (plus refrigeration time) **serves** 4
per serving 59kJ (14 cal); 0.1g total fat (0g saturated fat); 2.6g carbohydrate; 0.3g protein; 0.5g fibre

You can find lemon balm tea in most health food shops.

1 tablespoon lemon balm tea
½ cup loosely packed fresh mint leaves
1 litre (4 cups) water
2 tablespoons lemon juice
2 teaspoons white sugar

1 Combine tea, mint and the water in small saucepan; bring to a boil. Reduce heat; simmer, uncovered, 5 minutes.
2 Stand 1 minute; strain into large heatproof jug. Stir in juice and sugar; cool. Cover; refrigerate until cold then serve over ice.

spiced rose hip and hibiscus tea

preparation time 5 minutes
cooking time 2 minutes **serves** 4
per serving 13kJ (3 cal); 0g total fat (0g saturated fat); 0.7g carbohydrate; 0.1g protein; 0.2g fibre

2 rosehip and hibiscus tea bags
2 x 10cm strips orange rind
1 cinnamon stick
1 litre (4 cups) water

1 Combine ingredients in large heatproof jug; stand, uncovered, 2 minutes. Strain into another large heatproof jug.

iced lime and green tea

preparation time 5 minutes (plus refrigeration time) **serves** 4
per serving 13kJ (3 cal); 0g total fat (0g saturated fat); 0.1g carbohydrate; 0.1g protein; 0.2g fibre

2 green tea bags
4 slices lime
1 litre (4 cups) boiling water

1 Combine ingredients in large heatproof jug. Stand 5 minutes; remove tea bags and lime. Cover; refrigerate until cold.

iced lavender and lemon tea

preparation time 5 minutes (plus refrigeration time) **serves** 4
per serving 100kJ (24 cal); 0g total fat (0g saturated fat); 0.1g carbohydrate; 0.1g protein; 0.2g fibre

Dried lavender flowers are available from health food stores.

1 tablespoon dried lavender flowers
10cm strip lemon rind
1 litre (4 cups) boiling water
1 tablespoon honey

1 Combine lavender, rind and the water in large heatproof jug. Stand 5 minutes; strain into another large heatproof jug.
2 Stir in honey, cover; refrigerate until cold.

ginseng and star anise tea

preparation time 5 minutes **serves** 4
per serving 113kJ (27 cal); 0g total fat (0g saturated fat); 6.9g carbohydrate; 0.1g protein; 0.2g fibre

You can find ginseng for this recipe at all Asian grocers.

2 teaspoons ginseng
2 star anise
3 x 10cm strips orange rind
1 tablespoon honey
1 litre (4 cups) boiling water

1 Combine ingredients in large heatproof jug. Stand, uncovered, 5 minutes; strain into teapot or large heatproof jug.

did you know? A study into functional foods has stated that the health benefits of drinking black or green tea include possible reduced risk of coronary heart disease, as well as gastric, oesophageal and skin cancers. Tea also has been shown to help strengthen the immune system and possibly increase kilojoules burned during everyday activities.

glossary

artichoke, jerusalem neither from Jerusalem nor an artichoke, this crunchy, brown-skinned tuber tastes a bit like a water chestnut and belongs to the sunflower family. Eat raw in salads or cooked like potatoes.

barley a nutritious grain used in soups and stews.

> **pearl** has had the husk removed then been hulled and polished so that only the "pearl" of the original grain remains, much the same as white rice.

black beans also called turtle beans; they have a black skin, cream-coloured flesh and a sweet flavour; they are found in supermarkets, delicatessens and greengrocers. Not the same as chinese black beans, which are fermented soy beans.

blood orange a virtually seedless citrus fruit with blood-red rind and flesh; it has a sweet, non-acidic pulp and juice with slight strawberry or raspberry overtones.

bocconcini from the diminutive of "boccone", meaning mouthful in Italian; walnut-sized, baby mozzarella, a delicate, semi-soft, white cheese traditionally made from buffalo milk. Sold fresh, it spoils rapidly so will only keep, refrigerated in brine, for 1 or 2 days at the most.

broccolini a cross between broccoli and chinese kale, but milder and sweeter than broccoli. Each long stem is topped with a loose floret that looks like broccoli; it is completely edible.

buckwheat a herb in the same plant family as rhubarb; not a cereal so it is gluten-free. Available as flour (used for blini, pancakes and soba); ground (cracked) into coarse, medium or fine granules, which are called kasha and used similarly to polenta; or groats, the whole kernel sold roasted as a cereal product that forms the basis for a grain-and-vegetable main dish.

buk choy also known as bok choy, pak choi, chinese white cabbage or chinese chard; has a fresh, mild mustard taste. Use both stems and leaves, stir-fried or braised. *Baby buk choy*, also known as pak kat farang or shanghai bok choy, is much smaller and more tender than buk choy.

burghul also known as bulghur wheat; hulled, steamed, wheat kernels that, once dried, are crushed into various sized grains. Used in Middle Eastern dishes such as felafel, kibbeh and tabbouleh. Burghul is not the same as cracked wheat.

buttermilk originally the term given to the slightly sour liquid left after butter was churned from cream, today it is intentionally made from no-fat or low-fat milk to which specific bacterial cultures have been added during the manufacturing process. Despite its name, buttermilk is actually low in fat and is, therefore, a good substitute for dairy products such as cream or sour cream in some baking and salad dressings. It is available from the dairy department in supermarkets.

cannellini beans small white bean similar in appearance and flavour to great northern, navy or haricot beans. Available dried or canned, it's the bean used most often in ham and bean soup and baked beans.

chervil also known as cicily; mildly fennel-flavoured member of the parsley family with curly, dark-green leaves. Available both fresh and dried but, like all herbs, is best used fresh; its delicate flavour diminishes the longer it is cooked. It's one of the herbs usually included in the French staple *fines herbes* (along with chives, parsley and tarragon), and is used in the seasoning of omelettes and poached fish dishes.

chilli

> **chipotle** pronounced cheh-pote-lay. The name used for jalapeño chillies once they're dried and smoked. Having a deep, intensely smoky flavour, rather than a searing heat, chipotles are dark brown, almost black in colour and wrinkled in appearance. Available from specialty spice stores and delicatessens.
>
> **jalapeño** (hah-lah-pain-yo). Fairly hot, medium-sized, plump, dark green chilli; available pickled, canned or bottled, and fresh, from greengrocers.
>
> **red thai** also known as "scuds"; tiny, very hot and bright red in colour.

corn, baby can be purchased fresh from greengrocers, or in cans or jars.

craisins dried sweetened cranberries; used in cooking sweet or savoury dishes. Can usually be substituted for, or with, other dried fruit in most recipes.

gai lan also known as kanah, gai lum, chinese broccoli and chinese kale; appreciated more for its stems than its coarse leaves.

galangal a rhizome with a hot ginger-citrusy flavour; used similarly to ginger and garlic as a seasoning or an ingredient. Substitute fresh ginger if fresh galangal is unavailable.

garam masala a blend of spices including cardamom, cinnamon, cloves, coriander, fennel and cumin, roasted and ground together.

ginger

> **fresh** also known as green or root ginger; the thick gnarled root of a tropical plant. Ground ginger cannot be substituted for fresh ginger.
>
> **pickled** pink or red coloured; available, packaged, from Asian food shops. Pickled paper-thin shavings of ginger in a mixture of vinegar, sugar and natural colouring; most used in Japanese cooking.

ginseng the Chinese name for this sweet licorice-flavoured root is "human-shaped root" and some have extraordinarily human shapes. Ginseng is used in soups, for tea and as a medicinal. It's available in Asian markets and some health food stores.

harissa a North African paste made from dried red chillies, garlic, olive oil and caraway seeds. It is available ready-made from Middle Eastern food shops and some supermarkets.

horseradish a vegetable having edible green leaves but mainly grown for its long, pungent white root. Occasionally found fresh in specialty greengrocers and some Asian food shops, but is commonly purchased in bottles at the supermarket in two forms: prepared horseradish and horseradish cream. These cannot be substituted one for the other in cooking but both can be used as condiments. Horseradish cream is a commercially prepared creamy paste consisting of grated horseradish, vinegar, oil and sugar, while prepared horseradish is the preserved grated root.

kaffir lime leaf also also known as bai magrood. Sold fresh, dried or frozen; looks like two glossy, dark green leaves joined end to end, forming a rounded hourglass shape. A strip of fresh lime peel may be substituted for each kaffir lime leaf.

kecap manis a dark, thick, sweet soy sauce. Depending on the manufacturer, the sweetness is derived from the addition of either molasses or palm sugar when brewed.

kitchen string made from a natural product such as cotton or hemp that will neither melt nor affect the flavour of the food during cooking.

legumes the large plant family of seed pods, such as peas, lentils, chickpeas and beans; the common name of members of this family are pulses. Some can be eaten fresh, but most are usually dried then soaked before using in soups, stews and baked dishes.

lentils (red, brown, yellow) dried legumes often identified by, and named after, their colour; also known as dhal.

millet is a staple for almost a third of the world's population. It's prepared like rice by boiling it in water, and is used to make hot cereal and dishes like pilaf. Millet can be found in Asian markets and health food stores.

mince also known as ground meat, as in beef, veal, lamb, pork and chicken.

mirin a champagne-coloured Japanese cooking wine made from glutinous rice and alcohol. It is used expressly for cooking and should not be confused with sake. A seasoned sweet mirin, manjo mirin, made of rice, water, corn syrup and alcohol, is used in various Japanese dipping sauces.

miso fermented soybean paste. There are many types of miso, each with its own aroma, flavour, colour and texture; it can be kept, airtight, for up to a year in the fridge. Generally, the darker the miso, the saltier the taste and denser the texture. Salt-reduced miso is also available. Buy in tubs or plastic packs.

mushrooms

button small, cultivated, white mushrooms with a mild flavour.

enoki clumps of long, spaghetti-like stems with tiny, snowy white caps.

flat large, flat mushrooms with a rich, earthy flavour; ideal for filling and barbecuing. Are sometimes misnamed field mushrooms, which are wild mushrooms.

shiitake when fresh are also known as chinese black, forest or golden oak mushrooms; although cultivated, they have the earthiness and taste of wild mushrooms. Are large and meaty; often used as a substitute for meat in some Asian vegetarian dishes. When dried, they are known as donko or dried chinese mushrooms; rehydrate before use.

swiss brown also known as cremini or roman mushrooms, are light-brown mushrooms having a full-bodied flavour. Button or cup mushrooms can be substituted.

noodles

fresh rice also known as ho fun, khao pun, sen yau, pho or kway tiau. Can be purchased in strands of various widths or large sheets weighing about 500g, which are cut into the noodle-size desired. Chewy and pure white, they do not need pre-cooking before use.

hokkien also known as stir-fry noodles; fresh wheat noodles resembling thick, yellow-brown spaghetti needing no pre-cooking before use.

rice stick also known assen lek, ho fun or kway teow; they come in different widths (thin for soups, wide for stir-fries), but all should be soaked in hot water to soften.

rice vermicelli also known as sen mee, mei fun or bee hoon. Used throughout Asia in spring rolls and cold salads; similar to bean threads, only longer and made with rice flour instead of mung bean starch.

singapore pre-cooked wheat noodles best described as a thinner version of hokkien noodles.

soba thin, pale-brown noodle originally from Japan; made from buckwheat and varying proportions of wheat flour. Available dried and fresh, and in flavoured (for instance, green tea) varieties; eaten in soups, stir-fries and, chilled, on their own.

nori a type of dried seaweed used in Japanese cooking as a flavouring, garnish or for sushi. Sold in thin sheets, plain or toasted (yaki-nori).

oat bran the hard protective outer coating of the cereal grain normally removed from the kernel; is a high source of dietary fibre.

oatmeal a cereal product made from hulled oats. It is available in three textures: coarse, medium and fine.

oil

cooking spray we use a cholesterol-free cooking spray made from canola oil.

olive made from ripened olives. *Extra virgin* and *virgin* are the best, while *extra light* or *light* refers to taste, not fat levels.

peanut pressed from ground peanuts; the most commonly used oil in Asian cooking because of its high smoke point (capacity to handle high heat without burning).

walnut has a distinctive and nutty flavour, made from raw walnuts. Can be found in some supermarkets and most gourmet food stores. Store in a cool, dark place for up to 3 months; to prevent rancidity, keep it under refrigeration. Walnut oil is usually used in salad dressings combined with a less flavourful oil.

vegetable any of a number of oils sourced from plant rather than animal fats.

onions

green also known as scallion or, incorrectly, shallot; an immature onion picked before the bulb has formed, having a long, bright-green edible stalk.

red also known as red spanish, spanish or bermuda onion; a sweet-flavoured, large, purple-red onion.

shallots also called french shallots, golden shallots or eschalots; small, brown-skinned, elongated members of the onion family. Grows in tight clusters similar to garlic.

pancetta an Italian unsmoked bacon; pork belly cured in salt and spices then rolled into a sausage shape and dried for several weeks. Used as an ingredient rather than eaten on its own.

papaya, green unripe papaya; look for one that is hard and slightly shiny, proving it is freshly picked. Papaya will soften rapidly if not used within a day or two. Available at Asian food stores.

peppercorns, black are picked when the berry is not quite ripe, then dried until it shrivels and the skin turns dark-brown to black. Is the strongest flavoured of all the peppercorn varieties.

pepitas the pale green kernels of dried pumpkin seeds; they can be bought plain or salted.

pomegranate dark-red, leathery-skinned, fresh fruit about the size of an orange filled with hundreds of seeds, each wrapped in an edible lucent-crimson pulp having a unique tangy sweet-sour flavour.

preserved lemon salted lemons preserved in a mixture of olive oil and lemon juice; imparts a rich, salty-sour acidic flavour. Available from specialty food shops and delicatessens. Rinse well before using.

rice

- **arborio** small, round-grain rice well suited to absorb a large amount of liquid; especially suitable for risottos.
- **basmati** a fragrant long-grained white rice. It should be washed several times before cooking.
- **jasmine** fragrant long-grained rice; white rice can be substituted, but it will not taste the same.
- **koshihikari** grown in Australia from Japanese seed; a small, round-grain white rice perfect for sushi.
- **short-grain** fat, almost round, grain with a high starch content; tends to clump together when cooked.
- **wild rice blend** a packaged mixture of white long-grain and dark-brown wild rice. The latter is the seed of a North American aquatic grass, which has a distinctively nutty flavour and a crunchy, resilient texture.

rice vinegar a colourless vinegar made from fermented rice and flavoured with sugar and salt. Also known as seasoned rice vinegar; sherry can be substituted.

rocket also known as arugula, rugula and rucola; a peppery green leaf eaten raw or used in cooking. *Baby rocket leaves* are smaller and less peppery.

rosewater extract made from crushed rose petals; used in many desserts and sweetmeats (a small piece of something sweet such as candy or crystallised fruit). Don't confuse with rose essence, which is more concentrated.

saffron stigma of a member of the crocus family, available ground or in strands; imparts a yellow-orange colour to food once infused. The quality can vary greatly; the best is the most expensive spice in the world.

sake Japan's favourite wine, made from fermented rice, is used for marinating, cooking and as part of dipping sauces. If sake is unavailable, dry sherry, brandy, or vermouth can be substituted.

shallots *see onions*.

silver beet also known as swiss chard and, incorrectly, spinach; has fleshy stalks and large leaves.

spinach also known as english spinach and, incorrectly, silver beet. *Baby spinach leaves* are best eaten raw in salads; the larger leaves should be cooked until barely wilted.

star anise a dried star-shaped pod whose seeds have an astringent aniseed flavour; commonly used to flavour stocks and marinades.

sugar

- **brown** a very soft, finely granulated sugar retaining molasses for its characteristic colour and flavour.
- **caster** also known as superfine or finely granulated table sugar.
- **palm** also known as nam tan pip, jaggery, jawa or gula melaka; made from the sap of the sugar palm tree. Light-brown to black in colour and usually sold in rock-hard cakes; brown sugar can be substituted if palm sugar is unavailable.
- **white** coarse, granulated table sugar, also known as crystal sugar.

tahini sesame seed paste available from Middle Eastern food stores; often used in hummus and baba ghanoush.

tamarind the tamarind tree produces clusters of hairy brown pods, each of which is filled with seeds and a viscous pulp, that are dried and pressed into the blocks of tamarind found in Asian food shops. Has a sweet-sour, slightly astringent taste.

tamarind concentrate (or paste) the commercial result of the distillation of tamarind juice into a condensed, compacted paste.

thai basil also known as horapa; different from holy basil and sweet basil in both look and taste, having smaller leaves and purplish stems. It has a slight aniseed taste and is one of the identifying flavours of Thai food.

tofu also known as soybean curd or bean curd; an off-white, custard-like product made from the "milk" of crushed soybeans. Comes fresh as soft or firm, and processed as fried or pressed dried sheets. *Silken tofu* is not a type of tofu, but reference to the manufacturing process of straining soybean liquid through silk; this denotes best quality.

wakame pronounced wah-kah-meh; a deep green, edible seaweed popular in Japan and other Asian countries. It's used like a vegetable in soups and simmered dishes, as well as occasionally in salads. Wakame is available both in fresh and dried forms in Asian markets.

wasabi an Asian horseradish used to make the pungent, green-coloured sauce traditionally served with Japanese raw fish dishes; sold in powdered or paste form.

water chestnuts resemble true chestnuts in appearance, hence the English name. Small brown tubers with a crisp, white, nutty-tasting flesh. Their crunchy texture is best experienced fresh; however, canned water chestnuts are more easily obtained and can be kept for about a month in the fridge once opened. Used, rinsed and drained, in salads and stir-fries.

watercress also known as winter rocket; one of the cress family, a large group of peppery greens used raw in salads, dips and sandwiches, or cooked in soups. Highly perishable, so it must be used as soon as possible after purchase.

zucchini also known as courgette; small, pale- or dark-green, yellow or white vegetable belonging to the squash family. Harvested when young, its edible flowers can be stuffed and deep-fried or oven-baked to make a delicious appetiser.

conversion chart

MEASURES

One Australian metric measuring cup holds approximately 250ml; one Australian metric tablespoon holds 20ml; one Australian metric teaspoon holds 5ml.

The difference between one country's measuring cups and another's is within a two- or three-teaspoon variance, and will not affect your cooking results. North America, New Zealand and the United Kingdom use a 15ml tablespoon.

All cup and spoon measurements are level. The most accurate way of measuring dry ingredients is to weigh them. When measuring liquids, use a clear glass or plastic jug with the metric markings.

We use large eggs with an average weight of 60g.

DRY MEASURES

METRIC	IMPERIAL
15g	½oz
30g	1oz
60g	2oz
90g	3oz
125g	4oz (¼lb)
155g	5oz
185g	6oz
220g	7oz
250g	8oz (½lb)
280g	9oz
315g	10oz
345g	11oz
375g	12oz (¾lb)
410g	13oz
440g	14oz
470g	15oz
500g	16oz (1lb)
750g	24oz (1½lb)
1kg	32oz (2lb)

LIQUID MEASURES

METRIC	IMPERIAL
30ml	1 fluid oz
60ml	2 fluid oz
100ml	3 fluid oz
125ml	4 fluid oz
150ml	5 fluid oz (¼ pint/1 gill)
190ml	6 fluid oz
250ml	8 fluid oz
300ml	10 fluid oz (½ pint)
500ml	16 fluid oz
600ml	20 fluid oz (1 pint)
1000ml (1 litre)	1¾ pints

LENGTH MEASURES

METRIC	IMPERIAL
3mm	⅛in
6mm	¼in
1cm	½in
2cm	¾in
2.5cm	1in
5cm	2in
6cm	2½in
8cm	3in
10cm	4in
13cm	5in
15cm	6in
18cm	7in
20cm	8in
23cm	9in
25cm	10in
28cm	11in
30cm	12in (1ft)

OVEN TEMPERATURES

These oven temperatures are only a guide for conventional ovens. For fan-forced ovens, check the manufacturer's manual.

	°C (CELSIUS)	°F (FAHRENHEIT)	GAS MARK
Very slow	120	250	½
Slow	150	275-300	1-2
Moderately slow	160	325	3
Moderate	180	350-375	4-5
Moderately hot	200	400	6
Hot	220	425-450	7-8
Very hot	240	475	9

index

COOKBOOK HOLDERS

Keep your ACP cookbooks clean, tidy and within easy reach with a holder that carries up to 12 books

Book Holder Australia $13.10 (incl. GST). Elsewhere: $A21.95.

Mail or fax Photocopy and complete the coupon below and post to ACP Books Reader Offer, ACP Publishing, GPO Box 4967, Sydney NSW 2001, or fax to (02) 9267 4967.

Phone Have your credit card details ready, then phone 136 116 (within Australia) Mon-Fri, 8.00am-6.00pm; Sat, 8.00am-6.00pm.

Australian residents We accept the credit cards listed on the coupon, money orders and cheques.

Overseas residents We accept the credit cards listed on the coupon, drafts in $A drawn on an Australian bank, and also UK, NZ and US cheques in the currency of the country of issue. Credit card charges are at the exchange rate current at the time of payment.

Photocopy and complete coupon below

Mr/Mrs/Ms ______________________________

Address ______________________________

______________________ Postcode ____________

Country ______________ Phone (business hours) ______________

Email* (optional) ______________________________

Quantity ______________ Total cost $ ____________

I enclose my cheque/money order for __________ $ ____________

payable to ACP Magazines or please charge __________ $ ____________

to my: ☐ Bankcard ☐ Mastercard ☐ Visa ☐ American Express ☐ Diners Club

Expiry date ____________

Card number |_|_|_|_|_|_|_|_|_|_|_|_|_|_|_|_|

Cardholder's signature ______________________________

* By including your email address, you consent to receipt of any email regarding this magazine, and other emails which inform you of ACP's other publications, products, services and events, and to promote third party goods and services you may be interested in.
Please allow up to 30 days delivery within Australia. Allow up to 6 weeks for overseas delivery.
Offer expires 31/12/07 HLHE07

ACP Magazines Ltd Privacy Notice
This book may contain offers, competitions or surveys that require you to provide information about yourself if you choose to enter or take part in any such Reader Offer. If you provide information about yourself to ACP Magazines Ltd, the company will use this information to provide you with the products or services you have requested, and may supply your information to contractors that help ACP to do this. ACP will also use your information to inform you of other ACP publications, products, services and events. ACP will also give your information to organisations that are providing special prizes or offers, and that are clearly associated with the Reader Offer.
Unless you tell us not to, we may give your information to other organisations that use it to inform you about other products, services and events or who may give it to other organisations that may use it for this purpose. If you would like to gain access to the information ACP holds about you, please contact ACP's Privacy Officer at ACP Magazines Ltd, 54-58 Park Street, Sydney, NSW 2000.

☐ **Privacy Notice** Please do not provide information about me to any organisation not associated with this offer.